BEING CONSUMED

BEING CONSUMED

Economics and Christian Desire

William T. Cavanaugh

William B. Eerdmans Publishing Company
Grand Rapids, Michigan / Cambridge, U.K.

Published 2008 by

Wm. B. Eerdmans Publishing Co.

2140 Oak Industrial Drive N.E., Grand Rapids, Michigan 49505 /

P.O. Box 163, Cambridge CB3 9PU U.K.

Printed in the United States of America

27 26 25 24 23   19 20 21 22 23

Library of Congress Cataloging-in-Publication Data

Cavanaugh, William T.

Being consumed: economics and Christian desire / William T. Cavanaugh.

p.   cm.

Includes bibliographical references.

ISBN 978-0-8028-4561-0 (pbk.: paper)

1. Economics — Religious aspects — Christianity.

2. Desire — Religious aspects — Christianity.

3. Consumption (Economics) — Religious aspects — Christianity.

I. Title.

BR115.E3C38   2008

261.8′5 — dc22

2007044627

www.eerdmans.com

Contents

Introduction

Some Christians may be tempted to assume that economics is a discipline autonomous from theology. Many Christians, however, intuit that what we do with our money and our stuff should be directly informed by how we relate to God. God and Mammon are somehow contestants on the same playing field. Nevertheless, Christians of the latter kind tend to remain in a reactive posture. That is, we tend to take current economic realities as givens and then wonder what our stance should be when confronted by these givens. Are we for or against the free market? Should we not think of ourselves as consumers? Are we for or against globalization? How do we live in a world of scarce resources?

In the four brief chapters of this book, I deal with these basic matters of economic life: the free market, consumerism, globalization, and scarcity. In each chapter I use Christian resources to try to change the terms of the debate. In the first chapter, I use Augustine to argue that there is no point in being either for or against "the free market" as such. The key question is: When is a market free? In the second chapter, I discuss how, in the Eucharist, God forms us to consume rightly. In the third chapter, I argue that, rather than simply being for or against globalization, the church catholic should be about knowing how to be global and how to be local. Finally, in the fourth chapter, I show that life in Christ refuses to accept scarcity as a given. Taken as a whole, this book attempts to sketch out a view of everyday economic life with the use of Christian resources. I examine some pathologies of desire in contemporary "free-market economies," and display a positive vision of how the dynamics of desire in Christ can both form and be formed by alternative economic practices.

This book will be, I hope, a contribution to a kind of theological microeconomics. Rather than blessing or damning the "free market" as such, I want to focus our attention on concrete Christian attempts to discern and create economic practices, spaces, and transactions that are truly free. Christians are not faced with the choice of either accepting "the free market" as it is, or pinning our hopes on state intervention to bring freedom to the market. We might perhaps recognize, under certain circumstances, the usefulness of the state in mitigating the most egregious injustices of the market. But I argue that Christians themselves are called to create concrete alternative practices that open up a different kind of economic space — the space marked by the body of Christ.

In order to address the subject of economics from a theological point of view, we need to discuss the ends of human life, specifically the end of life in God. This means that we should not defer a discussion of the ends of human life in favor of a more formal discussion of whether the market performs best with or without state intervention. The key question in every transaction is whether or not the transaction contributes to the flourishing of each person involved, and this question can only be judged, from a theological point of view, according to the end of human life, which is participation in the life of God. This, in turn, means that a theological vision of economics cannot help but engage at the micro level, where particular kinds of transactions — those that really enhance the possibility of communion among persons and between persons and God — are to be enacted. For this reason, in every chapter I point to concrete examples of alternative economic practices in which Christians participate — businesses, cooperatives, credit unions, practices of consumption — that together mark out a vision for Christian economic life.

Those looking for a radical Christian alternative to the way things are might at this point be wondering if a certain kind of resignation underlies this project. Perhaps the era of grand revolutions has passed, and all we can hope for now, at the "end of history," is to create "niche markets" in which do-gooders can appease their consciences by making a few socially conscious purchases. I have no doubt that many, if not all, of the practices I mention in this book can be written into the grand narrative of capitalism. "Fair Trade" coffee, for example, can be read as simply showing the genius of the market to accommodate all kinds of preferences, including the preference to pay a bit more to support a poor farmer.

Christians, nevertheless, will narrate the Fair Trade movement differently, as the pursuit of one of the chief ends of human life, that is, communion with other persons. This is not the mere expression of a preference but the pursuit of an end that is objectively valid — that is, given by God, not simply chosen. If we are dealing with a liberal state that professes to be agnostic about the ultimate ends of human life, and if we are not willing to endorse the violent imposition of state socialism, then Christians who are called to witness to a different kind of economics have no choice but simply to enact this economics now, in history, beginning in the concrete, local experience of the church. There can be no resignation to the way things are. The church is called to be a different kind of economic space and to foster such spaces in the world. This does not mean a "sectarian" withdrawal from the world;

Christians are in constant collaboration with non-Christians in making such spaces possible. But there is simply no alternative to the actual creation of cooperatives, businesses, and other organisms that behave according to the logic of the gospel. The only alternative to blessing or damning "the free market" as such is to create really free markets, economic spaces in which truly and fully free transactions — as judged by the true *telos* of human life — can take place. The goal is indeed revolution, to transform the entirety of economic life into something worthy of God's children. But it is a revolution that cannot be imposed from above by force. It will only take place in the concrete transformation of transactions that enslave into transactions that are free.

I focus each chapter of this book on a set of binaries: negative freedom and positive freedom, detachment and attachment, the global and the local, scarcity and abundance. Chapter 1 challenges free-market ideology, which is concerned to proclaim the blessings of "the free market" and to warn against state intervention therein. In examining some of Milton Friedman's writings on freedom, I demonstrate some problems with this ideology, but I do not think there is any point in rejecting the free market as such. The crucial question is: When is a market free? In other words, how can we judge when any particular transaction is free? I reject the idea that a transaction is free just because it is not subject to state intervention or any other form of external coercion. We must give a fuller, more positive, account of freedom; and to do so from a Christian point of view, we must draw on theological resources. In this first chapter I use some of Augustine's writings on free will to show that real freedom must embrace the positive end *(telos)* of life in God. I show that a merely negative view of freedom, as in Friedman, lends itself to coercion. In the absence of any objective ends to which desire is directed, all that remains is the sheer arbitrary power of one will against another.

In Chapter 2, I examine the dynamics of attachment and detachment in consumer culture. Although consumerism is often equated with greed, which is an inordinate attachment to material things, I show that consumerism is, in fact, characterized by detachment from production, producers, and products. Consumerism is a restless spirit that is never content with any particular material thing. In this sense, consumerism has some affinities with Christian asceticism, which counsels a certain detachment from material things. The difference is that, in consumerism, detachment continually moves us from one product to another, whereas in Christian life, asceticism is a means to a greater attachment to God and to other people. We are consumers in the Eucharist, but in consuming the body of Christ we are transformed into the body of Christ, drawn into the divine life in communion with other people. We consume in the Eucharist, but we are thereby consumed by God.

In Chapter 3, I examine the binary concepts of global and local. I describe globalization as a kind of aesthetics, a way of looking at the world that produces and is produced by a certain kind of desire. Globalization claims to encourage a diversity of the particular and the local, both identities and products, but the proliferation of the particular and the local tends to be swallowed up into a universal gaze. Differences proliferate, but ultimately the differences do not matter; for the globalized desire, everything is available, but nothing matters. This applies equally to globalized economies and to globalized theologies, in which Jesus is just one exemplification of a more universal ultimate reality. However, the Christian response is not simply to reject the global for the local. I draw on theologian Hans Urs von Balthasar's analysis of Jesus Christ as the "concrete universal" to argue that Christ solves the problem of the global and the local — or the one and the many — in a satisfactory way. We are then called to realize the universal body of Christ in every particular and local exchange.

In Chapter 4, I address the question of scarcity, which is one of the fundamental loci of modern economics. The standard assumption of economists that we live in a world of scarce resources is not based simply on an empirical observation of the state of the world, but is based on the assumption that human desire is limitless. In a consumer culture we are conditioned to believe that human desires have no end and are therefore endless. The result is a tragic view of the world, a view in which there is simply never enough to go around, which in turn produces a kind of resignation to the plight of the world's hungry people. The Eucharist, by way of contrast, enacts a different story, a story of abundance: by being drawn into God's life, we radically call into question the boundaries between the haves and the have-nots.

In each chapter I connect theology to practice by briefly indicating some concrete examples of how God's economy is enacted by Christians and others on a daily basis. I point to consumer choices such as buying local goods, supporting producer-consumer cooperatives such as church-supported agriculture and Fair Trade, investing in banks that support grass-roots development, supporting gospel-inspired business models such as Focolare's Economy of Communion and the Mondragón Corporation, and attempting to overcome the passivity of consumption by making products of one's own. These examples are not meant to constitute an exhaustive treatment of alternative economic spaces in which Christians participate, but I hope they will provide inspiration for the Christian imagination to envision and enact new kinds of practices. Taken together, these examples indicate that the Christian vision of economics that animates this book is not impractical but may in fact be the most practical of all ways to live out the Christian life.

chapter 1

FREEDOM AND UNFREEDOM

There is a gap between dual perceptions of the market economy that seems to be getting wider in the age of globalization. On the one hand, we are told that we live in an era of unparalleled freedom of choice. As the last few state barriers to free markets crumble, we see an infinity of opportunities for work and consumption opening up all around us. On the other hand, there is a profound sense of resignation to fate in attitudes toward the market. The process of globalization seems to have advanced beyond anyone's control. Managers sigh that their decisions are subject to the impersonal control of "market forces." The popularity of *Dilbert* cartoons bespeaks a cynicism about the instrumentalized and bureaucratized nature of corporate employment. Consumers feel besieged by marketing and surveillance, and they feel powerless in the face of enormous transnational corporations that are disconnected from the communities where they live. We hear rumors that our shoes are made by chil-

Thanks to D. Stephen Long and Michael Naughton for their helpful comments on an earlier draft of this chapter.

dren and other exploited laborers, but we have no idea how we could begin to resist.

The argument of this chapter is that there is a fundamental connection between these two kinds of perception of the market. In the ideology of the free market, freedom is conceived as the absence of interference from others. There are no common ends to which our desires are directed. In the absence of such ends, all that remains is the sheer arbitrary power of one will against another. Freedom thus gives way to the aggrandizement of power and the manipulation of will and desire by the greater power. The liberation of desire from ends, on the one hand, and the domination of impersonal power, on the other, are two sides of the same coin.

If this is the case, then true freedom requires an account of the end *(telos)* of human life and the destination of creation. I use St. Augustine to help make this argument. There is no point to either blessing or damning the "free market" as such. What is required is a substantive account of the end of earthly life and creation so that we may enter into particular judgments of what kinds of exchanges are free and what kinds are not.

I. When Is a Market Free?

When is a market free? According to Milton Friedman, the central problematic of economics is how to ensure the cooperation of free individuals without coercion. The answer, says Friedman, was provided by Adam Smith, who saw that, in the absence of external coercion, two parties enter into exchanges because it will be mutually beneficial for them to do so, *"provided the transaction is bi-laterally voluntary and informed."*[1] No exchange will take place unless both parties benefit.

1. Milton Friedman, *Capitalism and Freedom* (Chicago: University of Chi-

Freedom and Unfreedom

So long as effective freedom of exchange is maintained, the central feature of the market organization of economic activity is that it prevents one person from interfering with another with respect to most of his activities. The consumer is protected from coercion by the seller because of the presence of other sellers with whom he can deal; the seller is protected from coercion by the consumer because of other consumers to whom she can sell; the employee is protected from coercion by the employer because of other employers for whom he can work, and so on. And the market does this impersonally and without centralized authority.[2]

State authority is necessary to maintain law and order and enforce contracts that are voluntarily entered into, but the state must not interfere in the market; in fact, the state may be called on to prevent such interference. According to Friedman, if individuals are voluntarily entering into exchanges from which both parties expect to benefit, then the market is free.

This is a fairly conventional definition of a free-market economy. It hinges on the insistence that exchanges be voluntary and informed. With regard to information, an exchange cannot be free if one party has deceived another, say, by selling the other a house without divulging a severe problem with termites. Barring such deception, however, Friedman is confident that the price system in a free-market economy transmits all the information needed to make exchanges informed. Indeed, "[t]he price system transmits only the important information and only to the people who need to know."[3] Producers of wood do not need to know

cago Press, 1962), p. 13; Milton and Rose Friedman, *Free to Choose* (New York: Avon Books, 1980), pp. xv-xvi.

2. Friedman, *Capitalism and Freedom*, pp. 14-15.
3. Friedman, *Free to Choose*, p. 7.

3

why demand for pencils has increased or even *that* it has increased. They only need to know that someone is willing to pay more for their product to increase production. At the other end, the increased price of pencils will tell the consumer to wear her pencil down to a stub before buying a new one. She doesn't need to know *why* the price of pencils has increased, only that it has.[4] Similar comments apply to the contract between employer and employee: the price system applies in equal measure because wages and salaries are the prices of labor, and the employer-employee relationship is an exchange of labor for money.

Besides being informed, a free-market exchange must also be voluntary. What this seems to mean, first, is an absence of external coercion. The chief culprit here is the state. In a free-market economy, the state does not interfere. No one threatens dire consequences if one party decides not to enter into a particular exchange. In a voluntary exchange, each party enters into the transaction in the expectation of gain and not in the fear of punishment. Second, then, voluntary exchanges are based on each party's desires. They need not want the same kinds of things: wrestling videos and rosaries can be freely exchanged for each other. There need be no agreement at all on the nature of desire for a voluntary exchange to take place. A market is free if people can satisfy their wants without harming others, even if there are utterly incommensurable ideas about what people ought to desire. As Friedman says, a free-market economy "gives people what they want instead of what a particular group thinks they ought to want. Underlying most arguments against the free market is a lack of belief in freedom itself."[5] Freedom itself is pursuing whatever you want without interference from others.

4. Friedman, *Free to Choose,* pp. 7-8.
5. Friedmam, *Capitalism and Freedom,* p. 15.

Freedom and Unfreedom

Two corollaries follow from this concept of voluntary exchange. The first is that freedom is defined negatively, that is, as freedom *from* the interference of others, especially from the state. Freedom is what exists spontaneously in the absence of coercion. This approach is agnostic about the positive capacities of each party to a transaction, for example, how much power or property each party has at his or her disposal. To be free, it suffices that there be no external interference. The second corollary is that a free market has no *telos,* that is, no common end to which desire is directed. Each individual chooses his or her own ends. As Friedrich Hayek says, "this recognition of the individual as the ultimate judge of his ends" does not mean there can be no common action among individuals, but the ends on which such actions are based are merely the "coincidence of individual ends."[6] "What are called 'social ends' are [from a free-market view] merely identical ends of many individuals — or ends to the achievement of which individuals are willing to contribute in return for the assistance they receive in the satisfaction of their own desires."[7] To claim that desires can be ordered either rightly or wrongly to objectively desirable ends has no place in a free market. To stake such a claim within the market itself would be to interfere in the freedom of the market. As Michael Novak says, democratic capitalism — of which a free market is a crucial component — is built on the explicit denial of any unitary order. There is no common *telos* or "sacred canopy" above the diversity of desires, only an "empty shrine" or "wasteland" where common goals used to stand.

6. Friedrich A. Hayek, *The Road to Serfdom* (Chicago: University of Chicago Press, 1944), p. 59.
7. Hayek, *Road to Serfdom,* p. 60.

The "wasteland" at the heart of democratic capitalism is like a field of battle, on which individuals wander alone, in some confusion, amid many casualties. Nonetheless, like the dark night of the soul in the inner journey of the mystics, this desert has an indispensable purpose. It is maintained out of respect for the diversity of human consciences, perceptions, and intentions. It is swept clean out of reverence for the sphere of the transcendent, to which the individual has access through the self, beyond the mediations of social institutions.[8]

The transcendent is not denied but preserved in the freedom of each individual to pursue the ends of his or her choice.

If ends are chosen and not received, on what basis are these choices of ends made? On the basis of "wants" or "preferences" or "desires." Where do these come from? Free-market economists are agnostic on this question. It may be unanswerable, and it does not matter anyway. Milton and Rose Friedman address a distinction sometimes made between the "real wants or desires of consumers" and artificial wants supposedly created by advertising. They believe that advertising succeeds not by creating artificial wants but by appealing to real wants. "Is it not more sensible to appeal to real wants or desires of consumers than to try to manufacture artificial wants or desires? Surely it will generally be cheaper to sell them something that meets wants they already have than to create an artificial want."[9] As an example, the Friedmans cite the success of automobiles that change models year after year over those, such as the Superba, that did not. If unchanging models were "what consumers *really* wanted, the com-

8. Michael Novak, *The Spirit of Democratic Capitalism* (New York: Simon and Schuster, 1982), pp. 54-55.
9. Friedman, *Free to Choose*, p. 214.

panies that offered that option would have prospered, and the others would have followed suit."[10] How do you tell the difference between real wants and artificial wants? Simply by seeing what people in fact choose. If they choose something, they must have a real want for it. Where do real wants come from? For the Friedmans, it doesn't matter. All that matters for a market to be free is that individuals have real wants and can pursue them without the interference of others, especially the state.

II. Augustine on Freedom and Desire

An examination of Christian thinking on voluntary action renders both of the above corollaries — that freedom is defined purely negatively and that freedom requires no objective ends — suspect. I will take as my principal guide St. Augustine of Hippo, arguably the classic source of Christian reflection on freedom and desire. Augustine was forced to wrestle with these questions in controversies with both the Pelagians, whose account of free will seemed to render God's grace unnecessary, and the Donatists, whose schism from the Catholic Church raised questions of using coercion to reunify the fold. These controversies may at first seem far removed from the dynamics of market economies, but Augustine represents the heart of Christian reflection on freedom and desire, and is thus directly implicated in any Christian attempt to answer the question "When is a market free?"

With regard to the first corollary identified above, freedom in Augustine's view is not simply the absence of external interference. Augustine's view of freedom is more complex: freedom is not simply a negative freedom *from*, but a freedom *for*, a capacity

10. Friedman, *Free to Choose*, p. 214 [italics in the original].

to achieve certain worthwhile goals. All of those goals are taken up into the one overriding *telos* of human life, the return to God. Freedom is thus fully a function of God's grace working within us. Freedom is being wrapped up in the will of God, who is the condition of human freedom. Being is not autonomous; all being participates in God, the source of being.

Autonomy in the strict sense is simply impossible, for to be independent of others and independent of God is to be cut off from being, and thus to be nothing at all. To be left to our own devices, cut off from God, is to be lost in sin, which is the negation of being. For the Pelagians, in order for humans to be convicted of sin and rewarded for righteousness, their freedom must be in some sense "external" to divine grace. Freedom then becomes a kind of human power, and sin is an exercise of that power. For Augustine, on the other hand, sin is not a power but a weakness. Augustine uses the metaphors of slavery and sickness to discuss the nature of sin. In his *Confessions* he says of his own condition, before his conversion, that he was "bound not by an iron imposed by anyone else, but by the iron of my own choice."[11] In his anti-Pelagian treatise, *The Spirit and the Letter,* he says: "How, if they are slaves of sin, can they boast freedom of choice?"[12] Or again, "by grace comes the healing of the soul from sin's sickness; by the healing of the soul comes freedom of choice."[13] Sin is not subject to free choice, properly speaking. The alcoholic with plenty of money and access to an open liquor store may, in a purely negative sense, be free from anything interfering with getting what he wants; but in reality he is profoundly unfree and cannot free himself. In or-

11. St. Augustine of Hippo, *Confessions,* trans. Henry Chadwick (Oxford: Oxford University Press, 1991), p. 140 [VIII.10].

12. Augustine, *The Spirit and the Letter,* para. 52, in *Augustine: Later Works,* ed. John Burnaby (Philadelphia: Westminster Press, 1955), p. 236.

13. Augustine, *The Spirit and the Letter,* p. 236.

der for him to regain freedom of choice, he cannot be left alone. He can only be free by being liberated from his false desires and being moved to desire rightly. This is the sense in which Augustine says "freedom of choice is not made void but established by grace, since grace heals the will whereby righteousness may freely be loved."[14] Freedom is something received, not merely exercised. Therefore, in order to determine whether a person is acting freely, we need to know much more than whether or not that person is acting on his or her desires without the interference of others. In Augustine's view, others are in fact crucial to one's freedom. A slave or an addict, by definition, cannot free himself or herself. Others from outside the self — the ultimate Other being God — are necessary to break through the bonds that enclose the self in itself. Humans need a community of virtue in which to learn to desire rightly.[15]

On display here is a fundamentally different view of desire from that of the Friedmans. Augustine does not assume that individuals simply have wants that are internally generated and that subsequently enter the social realm through acts of choice. Nor does he assume that desires are simply real because people have them, nor that what one *really* desires is fully transparent and accessible to one's own self. For Augustine, desire is a social production: desire is a complex and multidimensional network of movement that does not simply originate within the individual self but pulls and pushes the self in different directions from both inside and outside the person. In his famous examination of his theft of

14. Augustine, *The Spirit and the Letter*, p. 236.

15. In his *Confessions*, Augustine writes of the habits of the will that hold back his conversion even after his intellectual problems have found resolution. At that point there appeared to him a vision of Lady Continence, who showed him a multitude of holy men and women to serve as exemplars for him and as mediators of God's grace (*Confessions*, pp. 150-52).

some pears as an adolescent, Augustine repeatedly draws attention to the social nature of the act.

> Yet had I been alone I would not have done it — I remember my state of mind to be thus at the time — alone I never would have done it. Therefore my love in that act was to be associated with the gang in whose company I did it. Does it follow that I loved something other than the theft? No, nothing else in reality because association with the gang is also a nothing.[16]

Here Augustine points to the social nature of desire, the origination of desire from both inside and outside the individual self. Augustine also points to the unreality of his desire. The object of his desire, because it is not oriented to the true end of human life, is in reality a nothing. His desire is not endowed with reality simply because he experiences it and chooses on the basis of it. Furthermore, the whole affair — and the desire itself — is not simply transparent to us mortals whose bodies are battlegrounds of competing loves: "Who can untie this extremely twisted and tangled knot?" The answer is God. Only through the sheer grace of God is Augustine able to continue on to say, "My desire is for you." That is, his *real* desire is for God.[17]

All of this indicates that there are true desires and false desires, and we need a *telos* to tell the difference between them. The second corollary of free-market economics that I have identified above is that freedom is maximized in the absence of a common *telos*. A market is free if individuals are free to choose their own ends based on nothing more than their own wants.

16. Augustine, *Confessions,* p. 33.
17. Augustine, *Confessions,* p. 34.

On the contrary, in his controversy with the Donatists, Augustine argues that freedom in fact depends not on the autonomy of the will but on the end to which the will is moved. I do not wish to defend Augustine's justification for the use of civil authority to compel the Donatists to rejoin the Catholic fold. What is interesting about the way Augustine argues in this matter, however, is his conceptualization of the relationship between freedom and coercion. For Augustine, the most important question is not whether the will has been moved externally or internally; rather, the most important question is to what end the will has been moved.

Augustine acknowledges that no one can be forced to be good against his or her own will. Nevertheless, since he does not assume that mere negative freedom of the will from interference is a good end in itself, he believes that the individual will can be moved from outside itself to re-examine its ways.[18] According to Augustine, many of the Donatists had long been prevented from examining the Catholic case because of complacency, fear, ignorance, and indifference. Their wills had become entrenched in habit; they were "held prisoners by the force of old custom."[19] What was needed, therefore, was for their wills to be moved from without. Just as Christ "coerced" Paul to cause his conversion, God's grace often works on us for our own profit — despite our own will.[20] In Augustine's thought, we desperately need not to be left to the tyranny of our own wills. The key to true freedom is not just following whatever desires we happen to have, but cultivating the right desires. This means that the internal movement of the will is not a sufficient condition for freedom; we must con-

---

18. Augustine, *Letter 93,* in *The Political Writings of St. Augustine,* ed. Henry Paolucci (Chicago: Gateway Editions, 1962), p. 203.

19. Augustine, *Letter 93,* p. 205.

20. Augustine, *Letter 93,* pp. 193-94.

sider the end toward which the will is moved. The mere fact of one party moving another against its will does not solve this question: "What is important to attend to but this: who were on the side of truth, and who on the side of iniquity; who acted from a desire to injure, and who from a desire to correct what was amiss?"[21] In the case of the Donatists, the "whole question, therefore, is whether schism be not an evil work."[22] For this reason, according to Augustine, Christ said, "Blessed are those who are persecuted," and added "for righteousness' sake."[23] The cause of the persecution makes all the difference.

Does this mean that the end justifies the means? In places it seems as though Augustine is saying so.

> When good and bad do the same actions and suffer the same afflictions, they are to be distinguished not by what they do or suffer, but by the causes of each: *e.g.* Pharaoh oppressed the people of God by hard bondage; Moses afflicted the same people by severe correction when they were guilty of impiety: their actions were alike; but they were not alike in the motive of regard to the people's welfare, — the one being inflated by the lust of power, the other inflamed by love.[24]

Nevertheless, Augustine ultimately makes no separation of ends and means. He counsels moderation in dealing with the Donatists, and he refuses to allow deception in bringing them back into the fold. Furthermore, Augustine rejects the use of judicial torture in dealing with the Donatists, and he limits the means of punishment to be used to those available to school-

21. Augustine, *Letter 93*, p. 198.
22. Augustine, *Letter 87*, p. 190.
23. Augustine, *Letter 87*, p. 191.
24. Augustine, *Letter 93*, p. 195.

teachers — beating with canes. "For he whose aim is to kill is not careful how he wounds, but he whose aim is to cure is cautious with his lancet; for the one seeks to destroy what is sound, the other that which is decaying."[25] His images from education and medicine here are deliberate. In pedagogy, a teacher will often need to redirect the will of students, sometimes forcefully, in order for them to learn. In medicine, the healer must sometimes produce pain for the sake of healing. In both cases, however, the administrator's means must be proportionate to the end in order to achieve a good end.

I believe that Augustine was wrong in his choice of means for dealing with the Donatists; nonviolent witness is a far more faithful means of persuasion. Nonetheless, Augustine's broader point about the relationship of desire to ends is valid, and it goes to the heart of our discussion of the freedom of the free market. The point is this: the absence of external force is not sufficient to determine the freedom of any particular exchange. In order to judge whether or not an exchange is free, one must know whether or not the will is moved toward a good end. This requires some kind of substantive — not merely formal — account of the true end, or *telos,* of the human person. Where there are no objectively desirable ends, and the individual is told to choose his or her own ends, then choice itself becomes the only thing that is inherently good. When there is a recession, we are told to buy things to get the economy moving; *what* we buy makes no difference. All desires, good and bad, melt into the one overriding imperative to consume, and we all stand under the one sacred canopy of consumption for its own sake.

And yet, Augustine says, desire for objects that are cut free from their source and their end in God is ultimately the desire for

25. Augustine, *Letter 93,* p. 197.

nothing. Because choice itself is the only good, because desire is the only thing objectively desirable, desire becomes a desire for nothing. In Augustine's vision of the great chain of being, all things that exist are good, but only insofar as they participate in God, the source of their being and the source of all good. To pursue the lower things on the chain of being for their own sake, to forget their source and their final end, is to sever the link that holds them in being, at which point they begin to slide back into the nothingness from which the *creatio ex nihilo* summoned them.[26] For Augustine, sin is committed when "in consequence of an immoderate urge towards those things at the bottom end of the scale of good, we abandon the higher and supreme goods, that is you, Lord God, and your truth and your law."[27] This is not just a matter of wanting too much; it is a matter of wanting without any idea why we want what we want. To desire with no good other than desire itself is to desire arbitrarily. To desire with no *telos*, no connection to the objective end of desire, is to desire nothing and to become nothing. "I abandoned you to pursue the lowest things of your creation. I was dust going to dust."[28]

Augustine presents a remarkably sympathetic account of the person in this condition, for even in the pursuit of lower things, Augustine spies the inchoate groping for the true end of human life. Even murder is committed out of love, but it is love for some lower good that has become detached from its true end.[29] All such loves are disordered loves, loves looking for something

26. See Augustine's exposition of evil as the privation of good, and therefore as nothing, in *Confessions*, pp. 124-25.

27. Augustine, *Confessions*, p. 30.

28. Augustine, *Confessions*, p. 16. Augustine's ideas here are put into literary form in C. S. Lewis's *The Great Divorce*. In Lewis's hell, everything — including the inhabitants — exists as mere shadow, with no solid reality.

29. Augustine, *Confessions*, p. 30.

worth loving that is not just arbitrarily chosen: "I sought an object for my love; I was in love with love."[30] Augustine would have no problem recognizing the pathologies of twenty-first-century advanced industrial countries, in which it is estimated that an addiction to shopping claims more than 10 percent of the population, and 20 percent of women — more than drugs and alcohol combined.[31] A person buys something — anything — trying to fill the hole that is the empty shrine. And once the shopper purchases the thing, it turns into a nothing, and she has to head back to the mall to continue the search. With no objective ends to guide the search, her search is literally endless.

III. *Libido dominandi*

Even if Augustine is right about the need for objective ends to guide the will, the question remains: Who is to say what those ends are? There is no doubt that Augustine's view can be taken in a very paternalistic direction: "*We* know what you really want, and we are going to organize society accordingly." I do not wish to endorse such a view. This is the specter of a socialist command economy that free-market advocates rightly reject. Free-market advocates would prefer to have individuals make their own mistakes. That some will make bad choices is inevitable; but it is far better to give individuals the freedom to damn themselves than to subject everyone to a power that is no more guaranteed than any other individual will to choose well.

30. Augustine, *Confessions*, p. 35.
31. See, for example, Tracy McVeigh: "One in five women is a shopaholic" (*London Observer*, Nov. 26, 2000). A search for "shopaholics anonymous" on the web generated the following advertising message: "Buy and sell 'shopaholics anonymous' and millions of other items on eBay!"

Nevertheless, the idea that this kind of economy is free is also problematic. The problem with the "free-market" view is that it assumes that the abolition of objective goods provides the conditions for the individual will to function more or less autonomously. The reality, however, is quite different. For, as Augustine sees clearly, the absence of objective goods does not free the individual, but leaves him or her subject to the arbitrary competition of wills. In other words, in the absence of a substantive account of the good, all that remains is sheer arbitrary power, one will against another. This is what Augustine calls the *libido dominandi*, the lust for power with which Pharaoh was possessed. Without the idea that some goods are objectively better than others, the movement of the will can only be arbitrary. Persuasion in this context can only be the domination of one will over another: the will is moved by the greater force, not by any intrinsic attraction to the good. The difference between authority and sheer power has been eliminated.

In this section I wish to look at some of the ways that power actually operates in the market. In the absence of any objective concept of the good, sheer power remains. The prevailing models of business strategy recognize this fact and are unsentimental about it. For example, on the one hand, marketing is communicated to the broader public as the provision of information about products so that consumers may make choices that are both informed and voluntary. Here consumers are depicted as autonomous and rational, perfectly sovereign over their choices of products and ends. On the other hand, marketing is an in-house presentation to its practitioners and clients that it is a machine fully capable of creating desire and delivering it to its intended goal. These two aspects of marketing are two sides of the same coin; marketing can manipulate desire successfully in part because of its success in convincing the broader public of consumers that it is not manipulating their desires. Richard Ott's popular marketing text *Creating Demand* is one example of the two faces of marketing. His introduction extols the consumer as king and declares the impossibility of manipulating consumers. However, the rest of his book is a detailed analysis of how to use the latest in psychological research to create desires by targeting consumers' subconscious impulses.[32] This is not an isolated example. Businesses clearly expect more from the billions of dollars they spend on advertising/marketing than the mere purveying of objective information to the consumer.

In fact, most contemporary marketing is based not on providing information but on associating products with evocative images and themes not directly related to the product itself. Goods that cannot be commodified, such as self-esteem, love, sex, friendship, and success, are associated with products that bear little or no relationship to those goods. Marketers intensify the desire for such goods by calling into question the acceptability of the consumer,[33] what General Motors' research division — in a reference to changing car models each year — once called "the organized creation of dissatisfaction."[34] This shift in the twentieth century from product-oriented advertising to buyer-centered approaches has been extensively documented, and it is recognized not just by critics of the advertising industry but by its practitioners as well. As one marketer promises, advertising creates emotional bonds between consumers

32. Richard Ott, *Creating Demand* (Burr Ridge, IL: Irwin Professional Publishing, 1992), cited in Michael Budde, *The (Magic) Kingdom of God: Christianity and Global Culture Industries* (Boulder, CO: Westview Press, 1997), p. 39.

33. Budde, *(Magic) Kingdom of God,* p. 43.

34. Quoted in Erik Larson, *The Naked Consumer: How Our Private Lives Become Public Commodities* (New York: Henry Holt and Company, 1992), p. 20. See the Friedmans' reference above to yearly car model changes as reflecting the "real desires" of consumers (footnote 9 above).

and products; it is about "creating mythologies about their brands by humanizing them and giving them distinct personalities and cultural sensibilities."[35] The efficacy of these approaches is augmented by the fact that most of us believe ourselves to be immune to such approaches. This sense of immunity is fostered by an entire genre of anti-advertising advertising, which either "exposes" the process of advertising itself (Sprite: "Image is nothing. Obey your thirst.") or advances the notion that, by buying the product in question, you will not be conforming but rather following your own path (Taco Bell: "Think outside the bun.")

It is, of course, true that advertising does not work on each individual the way a lobotomy does. Tracing cause and effect is difficult. The individual does not react like a programmed zombie on being exposed to effective advertising. As Michael Budde puts it, being subjected to advertising is more akin to playing poker against an opponent who, unbeknownst to you, has already seen the hand you are holding — perhaps in a slightly blurred mirror. You still exercise free will, but the dynamics of power have shifted because the situation is set up to advance the interests of others.[36] This imbalance of power happens in two related ways. First, surveillance ensures that the balance of information is decidedly in favor of the marketer. Not only do marketers withhold information about a product from consumers, or divert their attention to evocative images unrelated to the product itself; they also gather extensive information about individual consumers and target their efforts based on this disequilibrium of knowledge. Erik Larson details this phenomenon in his book *The Naked Consumer: How Our Private Lives Become Public Commodities.* Larson began re-

35. *Marketing News,* Feb. 17, 1992, quoted in Budde, *(Magic) Kingdom of God,* p. 38.
36. Budde, *(Magic) Kingdom of God,* p. 42.

search for the book when, a few days after the birth of his second daughter, a sample of Luvs diapers showed up on his doorstep, courtesy of the Procter & Gamble Corporation. His older daughter had already received birthday greetings, just days before turning one year old, from a marketer on behalf of several corporations, such as Revlon and Kimberly-Clark, who were selling toddler-related merchandise. Larson describes how information on our purchasing patterns, births, deaths, political views, educational levels, credit histories, pet ownership, hobbies, illnesses, and so on is harvested from credit-card records, bank statements, hospital records, websites visited, answers to surveys, frequent-buyer cards — even filmed records of our shopping habits in stores. Such surveillance has become incredibly sophisticated. A flyer for "OmniVision," a system developed by the consumer intelligence service of Equifax, boasts, "We think we know more about your own neighborhood than you do, and we'd like to prove it!"[37]

The second way marketers produce an imbalance of power is through the use of the information gathered from surveillance to saturate the social environment of consumers. The average person is exposed to thousands of advertising images every week. Virtually everywhere we look or listen — television, radio, websites, newspapers, magazines, billboards, junk mail, movies, videos, t-shirts, buses, hats, cups, pens and pencils, gas-pump handles, walls of public restrooms — is saturated with advertising. As one observer puts it, "What the record reveals is an almost total takeover of the domestic informational system for the purposes of selling goods and services."[38] To pretend, as Friedman does,

---

37. Larson, *Naked Consumer,* p. 58. An advertisement for Aristotle Industries says: "We can't tell you what they eat for dinner. But we can tell you where they live. And their phone number, who they live with, whether they have voted, and much, much more" (quoted in Larson, p. 3).

38. Herbert Schiller, quoted in Budde, *(Magic) Kingdom of God,* p. 33.

that the consumer simply stands apart from such pervasive control of information is to engage in fantasy.

Marketing is not the only area in which the logic of sheer power is manifest. Another is the concentration of power in enormous transnational corporations through mergers and acquisitions. The last two decades have seen an intensifying of mergers and acquisitions as large corporations seek to outdo their rivals through the increase of their size and market power. The result is such behemoths as AOL Time Warner and ExxonMobil. In industry after industry, a few huge corporations dictate patterns of production and consumption. In the meatpacking industry, for example, four giants handle 80 percent of the beef production in the United States, leaving small farmers and ranchers powerless to have any input into pricing or even how their cattle are raised. Myriad independent bookstores and department stores have shut down in the face of the advance of Barnes & Noble and Wal-Mart. Some argue that here the sovereign consumers have spoken: they simply prefer Barnes & Noble and Wal-Mart to smaller, less "efficient" operations. But if that's the case, king and queen consumer have paradoxically used their freedom to restrict their freedom, since now there are fewer choices available, and they are increasingly faced with the prospect of frequenting the same few chain stores whether they like it or not. Rather than celebrating the growth of enormously powerful corporations as the manifestation of consumer freedom, it is more realistic to examine the ability of sheer concentrated economic power to control patterns of consumption.

More severe than the asymmetrical power relations between corporation and consumer are the disparities of power in the exchange between employer and employee. In 1980 the average CEO made 42 times what the average production worker made; by 1999 that ratio had risen to 475 to 1, and it continues to rise.[39] Why do executives pay themselves so much? In part, because they can. Top executives serve on each other's boards of directors, and there is an expectation that they will keep up with increases in each other's pay packages. As the owners of capital have gained power, labor has lost power. Only 13 percent of American workers now belong to unions, and "Right to Work" legislation in twenty-nine states has made union organizing extremely difficult. A crucial factor in the atrophying of labor power in the United States has been the ability and willingness of corporations to shift production overseas, where they can and do pay wages as low as 30 cents an hour. Capital can move freely across national borders, but labor cannot. Factory workers in Massachusetts know that the threat that owners can move operations to El Salvador or China hangs over every negotiation with management, and the mere existence of such a threat suffices to weaken their bargaining power.

"Rosa Martinez produces apparel for US markets on her sewing machine in El Salvador. *You* can hire her for 33 cents an hour." So goes an advertisement, paid for by the U.S. Agency for International Development, in the textile trade journal *Bobbin*.[40] Why do companies pay such wages? Again, because they can. Transnational corporations are able to shop around the globe for the most advantageous wage environments, that is, those places where people are so desperate that they must take jobs that pay extremely low wages, in many cases wages insufficient to feed and house themselves and their dependents. In other words, it is considered good business practice to maximize the disparity of power between employer and employee in order to increase the profit

39. Michael J. Naughton, "The 'Stumbling and Tripping' of Executive Pay," *New Oxford Review* 68, no. 11 (Dec. 2001): 27-28.

40. Eric Bates, "Losing Our Shirts," *The Independent* (Durham, NC), April 6, 1994.

margin of the corporation. All of this is done in the name of "free" trade. As Augustine saw, in the absence of any substantive ends, what triumphs is the sheer lust for power. The one and only end is profit, the aggrandizement of the corporation — in short, naked power. This end is served precisely by the minimization of the employees' freedom.

"Because they can" is not the end of the story, however, for most managers of corporations would reply "because we must." There is a deeper sense in which managers act as they do because they feel compelled to do so. When managers lament the displacement and suffering caused by closing factories that pay living wages and opening others that do not, they are not just being disingenuous, nor are people who make such decisions *ipso facto* bad people. When they blame the move on necessity, they recognize a very real sense that the "free" market does not leave them free to act in ways they might believe are more just. In their search for cheap labor, managers often appeal to a sense of fate. They feel they have no choice in the matter, because they assume that, given the prevailing logic of free exchange, consumers will want to maximize their own gain in any transaction by paying the lowest price possible for a product. In a world of consumption without ends, it is assumed that the consumer will want to maximize his or her own power at the expense of the laborer, and the manager does not feel free to resist this logic, lest his or her own corporation fall victim to competition from other corporations that are better positioned to take advantage of cheap labor.

More than consumers, however, it is stockholders who drive the search for cheap labor. As Peter Drucker, Michael Naughton, and others have observed, over the last twenty years the tremendous concentration of stock in institutional investment plans — mutual funds, pension plans, insurance companies, and so forth — has shifted the power dynamics of publicly traded corporations. Institutional investors have put tremendous pressure on executives to maximize returns for their clients. At the same time, offering stock options to executives has been the favored tool for ensuring that the interests of the executives and those of the stockholders coincide. As a result of this shift of power, executives have strong incentives to favor the concerns of stockholders over those of other stakeholders, such as employees and their families and their communities.[41] Who owns corporations — the question of property, concerning which Friedman and others are generally agnostic — plays a crucial role in the dynamics of power.

When market forces alone are not enough to discipline the labor force, political coercion has often been brought to bear, supposedly on behalf of protecting free markets from interference. As the examples of China, South Korea, Singapore, Taiwan, and Myanmar indicate, authoritarian regimes are perfectly compatible with "free"-market economies, where a disciplined labor force is considered attractive to business. The economies of many Latin American nations were "freed" of state interference through a series of military dictatorships in the 1970s and 1980s. As Uruguayan writer Eduardo Galeano says about this period, "People were in prison so that prices could be free."[42] Milton Friedman himself made a highly publicized visit to General Pinochet's Chile in 1975 to help guide the reconstruction of the economy under Chilean economists known as "Los Chicago Boys," who had been students of Friedman and Arnold Harberger at the University of Chicago. In published remarks, Friedman counseled General Pinochet to ignore his image

41. Naughton, "'Stumbling and Tripping,'" pp. 27-31.
42. Eduardo Galeano, quoted in Lawrence Weschler, *A Miracle, A Universe: Settling Accounts with Torturers* (New York: Pantheon Books, 1990), p. 147.

abroad as an abuser of human rights and to focus instead on curing Chile of "statism."[43] Friedman also declared publicly that the Chilean economy needed "shock treatment."[44] To those thousands subject to torture by electroshock under Pinochet, Friedman's words were a chilling confirmation of the link between the discipline of labor and the freeing of capital.

IV. Judging When a Market Is Free

Is Rosa Martinez free? If we take Friedman's definition at face value, then we might answer yes. Her decision to take a job making clothes for American markets would presumably be both informed and voluntary, provided she was not deceived about the kind and amount of work she would be doing, or about the hourly amount she would be paid. Presumably no one would force her to take the job, and no one would prevent her from leaving it. Both Rosa Martinez and her employer would enter into this exchange in the expectation of benefiting from it. The employer would expect to increase profits by paying low wages, and Rosa Martinez would expect an improvement over starvation.

The problem with this view is that it pretends to be blind to the real disparity of power at work here while simultaneously stripping away the ability to judge an exchange on the basis of *anything but* sheer power, since any *telos,* or common standard of good, has been eliminated from view. Nothing necessarily connects the employer's desires to Rosa Martinez's desires. In Friedman's view, to ask whether this exchange serves the common good, or if it is just, is irrelevant to the question of whether or not

43. "El consejo del professor," *Ercilla* (April 2, 1975): 19-22.

44. Pamela Constable and Arturo Valenzuela, *A Nation of Enemies: Chile under Pinochet* (New York: W. W. Norton & Company, 1991), p. 170.

the exchange is free. We may only appropriately ask whether both parties are entering into the exchange expecting to gain something for their own individual interests that they would not have gained had they not entered into the exchange. Considerations of goodness and justice only seem to apply to the capitalist system as a whole. Friedman and other free-market advocates argue that capitalism as such is the best system based on its ability to give people what they want. A system that is allegedly based on individual rights is thus ironically justified by a utilitarian justification of the system as a whole, to which individuals and their freedom are sacrificed.

Some free-market advocates may wish to argue, on the other hand, that Rosa Martinez's exchange with her employer is not free, but that it is an aberration in the free-market system that will work itself out if the market mechanism is given time to operate. Similar claims could be made for all the examples I gave above under the heading *Libido dominandi*. That is, none of these are examples of the true functioning of the free market, and the market mechanism will protect against coercion if it is given time and allowed to function without interference.

However, in order to judge which exchanges are truly free and which ones are not, one must abandon Friedman's purely negative and functionalist approach to freedom and have some positive standard by which to judge. For example, if we admit that Rosa Martinez's exchange with her employer is voluntary and informed, yet still want to claim that it is not truly free, we must be able to muster an argument based on some standard of human flourishing and the ends of human life that are being violated by her working for less than a living wage. In other words, once we admit that freedom defined strictly negatively is inadequate, we are pushing ourselves toward the recognition that Augustine was right; to speak of freedom in any realistic and full sense is necessarily to engage the question of the true ends of human life. Yet such ends are precisely what free market advocates would banish from the definition of the free market. To enter into judgments about the freedom of particular exchanges, we must abandon Friedman's definition of a free market, and we must also abandon any claims for the goodness of "*the* free market" as such. There is no point to claiming that "capitalism produces freedom" unless one wants to claim that "any economic exchange that produces freedom is capitalism," in which case one has simply uttered a tautology. The key point is that the freedom of each economic exchange is subject to judgment based on a positive account of freedom, which must take into account the good ends of human life.

Let us consider some examples. Reporter Bob Herbert visited a factory in El Salvador that makes jackets for the Liz Claiborne line of clothing. The jackets sell for $178 each in the United States; the workers who make them earn 77 cents per jacket, or 56 cents an hour. The factory is surrounded by barbed wire and armed guards. A worker interviewed after her 12-hour shift told of being unable to feed herself and her three-year-old daughter adequately. Her daughter drinks coffee because they cannot afford milk; both mother and daughter suffer fainting spells. David Wang, president of Mandarin Company, which runs one of the plants in El Salvador, admitted to Herbert that the wages are inadequate: "If you really ask me, this is not fair." But then he went on to offer a lesson in "free" trade. "In the United States, if you want to buy a Honda Civic, you can shop around and always you will find cheaper ones." This is what the clothing companies were doing, according to Wang. "They are shopping around the whole world for the cheapest labor price."[45]

45. Bob Herbert, "In maquiladora sweatshops: Not a living wage," *Minneapolis Star Tribune*, Oct. 22, 1995.

Contrast this situation with the Spain-based Mondragón Cooperative Corporation, which was founded by Basque priest José Maria Arizmendiarrieta in 1956. Mondragón employs 60,000 people and has annual sales of manufactured goods in excess of $3 billion. What makes Mondragón extraordinary is that it is based on the principles of distributism: this idea — based on papal social teaching and promoted by Hilaire Belloc, G. K. Chesterton, and others — is that a just social order can only be achieved through just distribution of property and a recognition of the dignity of labor. Mondragón is entirely worker-owned and worker-governed, and it is based on a system of one vote per worker. At Mondragón they believe that labor hires capital, instead of capital hiring labor. Their capital comes largely from a credit union that is supported by workers and the community. The highest-paid employee can make no more than six times what the lowest-paid makes; 10 percent of surpluses are given directly to community development projects. Not only is the company successful and laborers highly satisfied with their work, but the communities in which Mondragón plays a significant part enjoy lower crime rates, lower rates of domestic violence, higher rates of education, and better physical and emotional health than neighboring communities.[46]

By Friedman's standards, both the Salvadoran textile worker and the worker at Mondragón are free. If we allow ourselves to judge freedom on the basis of the true ends of human life, however, it becomes obvious that the Salvadoran woman is little better than enslaved and that the Mondragón worker is afforded

---

46. Race Mathews, "Mondragon: Past Performance and Future Potential," paper presented at the Kent State University Capital Ownership Group Conference, Washington, DC (Oct. 2002). This paper can be found at http://cog.kent.edu/Author/Author.htm. More information on Mondragon is available at the company's website, www.mondragon.mcc.es.

the opportunity for true freedom. We must make particular judgments like this if we are not to use "freedom" as an empty slogan to cover over the depredations of naked power. Mondragón is founded on the recognition that true freedom requires a careful consideration of what is required for human flourishing, which requires consideration of the ends of being human. As Belloc said, "Economic freedom can only be a good if it fulfills some need in our nature."[47]

Economic freedom is in our eyes a good. It is among the highest of temporal goods because it is necessary to the highest life of society through the dignity of man and through the multiplicity of his action, in which multiplicity is life. Through well-divided property alone can the units of society react upon the State. Through it alone can a public opinion flourish. Only where the bulk of the cells are healthy can the whole organism thrive. It is therefore our business to restore economic freedom through the restoration of the only institution under which it flourishes, which institution is Property.[48]

The link between property and freedom is a crucial one. Free-market advocates tend to be agnostic on the question of ownership: barring external interference, an exchange is formally free even if the only thing a person has to exchange is his or her labor. But as the example of Rosa Martinez makes plain, having no ownership of anything can make one little better than a wage slave. For much of the Catholic tradition on the subject of property, going back to Aquinas and beyond, the ownership of prop-

47. Hilaire Belloc, *The Restoration of Property* (New York: Sheed & Ward, 1936), p. 21.
48. Belloc, *Restoration of Property*, p. 27.

erty is natural to human beings and allows them to develop their own capacities.[49] As Belloc says, property is thus essential to human freedom. But he does not construe freedom negatively here. The ownership of property is not about power, and the wide distribution of property is not about a greater equilibrium of power. Rather, property has an end, which is to serve the common good. The universal destination of all material goods is in God. As Aquinas says, we should regard property as a gift from God, a gift that is only valid if we use it for the benefit of others.[50] Thus Aquinas sanctions private ownership only insofar as it is put to its proper end, which is the good of all: "Man ought to possess external things, not as his own, but as common, so that, to wit, he is ready to communicate them to others in their need."[51] Absent such a view of the true end of property, freedom means being able to do whatever one wants with one's property, and property can thus become nothing more than a means of power over others.

Let us consider two more examples, this time having to do directly with consumption. When one buys a steak at a large chain grocery store, according to Friedman, all the information one needs in order to make a free decision — assuming that the steak is not simply defective or contaminated — is conveyed by the price. The true story behind the shrink-wrap, however, is more consequential than Friedman would have us believe. A calf might spend the first few months of its life eating grass on the range, but typically the rest of its short life is spent in a feedlot, ankle deep in manure. By nature, cattle are equipped to turn the grass that grows naturally on arid land into high-quality protein. However, allowing cattle to graze is considered inefficient these days, be-

49. St. Thomas Aquinas, *Summa Theologiae*, II-II.66.1.
50. Aquinas, *Summa*, II-II.66.1ad2.
51. Aquinas, *Summa*, II-II.66.2.

cause it takes too long. Today's beef cattle in the United States go from 80 to 1200 pounds in just fourteen months on a crash diet of corn, protein supplements, and drugs. They are given hormone implants (banned in Europe) to promote growth. Their calories come from corn, which is cheap and convenient but depends on the use of lots of petroleum products, and wreaks havoc on their ruminant digestive system, which is designed for grass. The only way to keep cattle from dying of bloating, acidosis, or abscessed livers as they fatten up on a grain diet is to give them steady doses of antibiotics. Still, many strains of bacteria survive. In the past, we could count on the fact that such bacteria, raised in a cow's neutral-pH digestive tract, would be killed off by the acids in the human stomach. But now that the cow's digestive tract has been acidified by a corn diet, acid-tolerant strains such as E. coli have developed; when those are found in our food, they can kill us. When the cattle are slaughtered, they are caked with feedlot manure, which is where the E. coli reside. Rather than altering beef cattle's diet or keeping them from living in their own feces or slowing down the processing speed of the slaughter lines, all of which are considered inefficient and impractical, processors spray the meat with disinfectant solution and irradiate it. Then they shrink-wrap it and send it to your local supermarket.[52]

The meat is cheap, but the social costs are not included in the price. Each head of cattle requires about 284 gallons of oil in its lifetime. As Michael Pollan says, "We have succeeded in industrializing the beef calf, transforming what was once a solar-powered ruminant into the very last thing we need: another fossil-fuel machine."[53] Runoff from the petroleum-based fertilizer has traveled

52. Michael Pollan, "Power Steer," *New York Times Magazine*, March 31, 2002.

53. Pollan, "Power Steer," p. 71.

down the Mississippi and created a 12,000-square-mile "dead zone" in the Gulf of Mexico. Extensive use of antibiotics has led to resistant strains of bacteria. And scientists believe that hormone use has contributed to dropping human sperm counts and sexual abnormalities in fish. One cattleman interviewed by Pollan said: "I'd love to give up hormones. If the consumer said, 'We don't want hormones,' we'd stop in a second. The cattle could get along better without them. But the market signal's not there, and as long as my competitor's doing it, I've got to do it, too."[54] But it is difficult to imagine how this signal would be generated, because the system is designed to keep the origins of beef a mystery to the consumer. So the cattleman continues to feel coerced into using hormones.

Contrast this to the Zweber Farm in Elko, Minnesota. When I buy beef from Jon and Lisa Zweber, I know that it is grass-fed, raised on pastureland behind their house. The Zwebers use no hormones or antibiotics in their operation. When I buy beef from them, it is a truly free exchange. All the information I need is available and transparent, and the exchange contributes to the flourishing of the Zwebers, their local community, my family, the cattle, and the environment. My exchange with the supermarket is less than free, because the information I need is not readily available to me. Before I read Michael Pollan, I had only the vaguest sense of how beef is typically raised. The ranchers and feedlot workers chafe under the compulsion of market forces beyond their control, and all the while their profit margins are squeezed ever tighter by the four conglomerates that dominate the meatpacking industry. And the overall effect of the system on the environment and on rural communities has been devastating.

54. Pollan, "Power Steer," p. 51.

V. Conclusion

Is this a call, then, for state intervention in the market? No. It is a false dichotomy to limit the possibilities to either requiring state intervention or blessing the unfettered reign of corporate power. Neither state intervention nor its absence ensures the freedom of a market. There is no point in making broad utilitarian claims about the benefits of "*the* free market" as if we could identify a market as "free" merely by the absence of restraint on naked power. Giving free rein to power without ends is more likely to produce unfreedom than to produce freedom. There is simply no way to talk about a really free economy without entering into particular judgments about what kinds of exchange are conducive to the flourishing of life on earth and what kinds are not. Though my purpose in this chapter has not been to go into detail about the specific ends of human work and material possessions, the Christian tradition provides a wealth of reflection on these matters.[55] I believe it would be counterproductive to expect the state to attempt to impose such a direction on economic activity. What is most important is the direct embodiment of free economic practices. From a Christian point of view, the churches should take an active role in fostering economic practices that are consonant with the true ends of creation. This requires promoting economic practices that maintain close connections among capital, labor, and communities, so that real communal discernment of the good can take place. Those are the spaces in which true freedom can flourish.

---

55. For example, the Catholic social encyclicals *Laborem Exercens, Quadragesimo Anno, Gaudium et Spes,* and others.

chapter 2

DETACHMENT AND ATTACHMENT

I n January 2005, a twenty-year-old Nebraska college student
auctioned off advertising space on his forehead. The winning
bid was over $37,000. For that princely sum, the young man spent
thirty days with a temporary tattoo on his forehead extolling the
virtues of a snoring remedy. Although his actual forehead would
be seen by a limited number of people, the manufacturer of the
product hoped to benefit by the worldwide publicity that the human ad campaign generated. The human billboard himself was
quoted as saying, "The way I see it I'm selling something I already
own; after thirty days I get it back."[1]

It would be easy to approach this story — and the subject of
this chapter, consumerism — with some stern finger-wagging
about the greed of people these days. "People will do anything for
money. Everybody wants more, and nobody wants to share with
those who have less. The world would be a better place if we all

---

1. "Man auctions ad space on forehead," BBC News, 10 Jan. 2005, at: http://
news.bbc.co.uk/1/hi/technology/4161413.stm. For information on the winning
bid, see Ina Steiner, "No Snooze for this eBay Auction: Ad Space Wins $37,375
Bid," AuctionBytes.com, January 25, 2005, at: http://auctionbytes.com/cab/
abn/y05/m01/i25/s07.

shared." And so on. But what makes consumer culture worth talking about from the point of view of moral theology is not primarily greed. The Nebraska man pulled this stunt to pay for his college education, not apparently out of plain greed. What is interesting about this story for our purposes is the way it illustrates something more basic about a consumer culture: its ability to turn virtually anything into a commodity, that is, into something that can be bought and sold.

The Christian tradition has always condemned greed (also called avarice). Jesus denounces storing up treasures on earth (Matt. 6:19-21); Paul attacks greed as a form of idolatry (Col. 3:5); Pope Gregory the Great included avarice in his list of seven deadly sins, which would serve over the centuries as a catalogue of perils for the soul to avoid.[2] Greed usually signifies an inordinate attachment to money and things. We think of the miser counting his money and storing it in the bank, or we picture the person reveling in her possessions, obsessed with stuffing her big house or houses with more things. But this view of greed does not really capture the spirit of our consumer economy. Most people are not overly attached to things, and most are not obsessed with hoarding riches. Indeed, the United States has one of the lowest savings rates of any wealthy country, and we are the most indebted society in history. What really characterizes consumer culture is not attachment to things but detachment. People do not hoard money; they spend it. People do not cling to things; they discard them and buy other things.

In a consumer society, detachment occurs in both selling and buying, and *anything* can be sold: healthcare, space, human blood, names ("Tostitos Fiesta Bowl"), adoption rights, water,

2. Henry Fairlie, *The Seven Deadly Sins Today* (Notre Dame, IN: University of Notre Dame Press, 1978), p. 12.

genetic codes, the rights to emit pollutants into the air, the use of one's own forehead. The Nebraska man describes himself as the "owner" of his forehead, which he can sell and get back. Consumerism is the remarkable ability to be detached even from those things, such as our foreheads, to which we are most obviously attached. But the detachment of consumerism is not just the willingness to sell anything. The detachment of consumerism is also a detachment from the things we buy. Our relationships with products tend to be short-lived: rather than hoarding treasured objects, consumers are characterized by a constant dissatisfaction with material goods. This dissatisfaction is what produces the restless pursuit of satisfaction in the form of something new. Consumerism is not so much about having more as it is about having something else; that's why it is not simply *buying* but *shopping* that is the heart of consumerism. Buying brings a temporary halt to the restlessness that typifies consumerism. This restlessness — the moving on to shopping for something else, no matter what one has just purchased — sets the spiritual tone for consumerism.

Consumerism is an important subject for theology because it is a spiritual disposition, a way of looking at the world around us that is deeply formative. In many ways, consumerism has affinities with the traditional Christian view of how we should regard material things. We will need to explore where consumerism and Christianity converge and where they part ways. In the first section of this chapter, I want to examine some of the economic conditions that typify consumerism and its detachment from production, producers, and products. In the second section, I will look at consumerism as moral formation and compare it with some themes from Christian moral theology. In the third section, I will explore the Eucharist as a Christian practice that offers an alternative way to practice consumption.

I. Detachment

Some critiques of consumerism are content to complain about the greed and materialism of the present age: people have abandoned God and the higher, more spiritual values of life for the base pleasures of material objects. There may be some truth to these complaints, but they miss the mark in at least two ways. First, they set up a false dichotomy between the spiritual and the material. In the Christian tradition, which believes that God became flesh (John 1:14), the material world is sanctified and charged with spiritual significance. The Christian is not meant to choose between God and the creation, because all of creation sings of the glory of God. In the Catholic tradition especially, the sacraments show us how we encounter God in everyday material elements. The second problem with such a critique of people's values is that most people do not simply choose material goods over spiritual values. The person who deliberately decides to become a hedonist and materialist is rare. Even pop singer Madonna, the self-declared "Material Girl," is involved in spirituality, a de-Judaized version of the ancient Jewish mystical practice called Kabbalah. Consumerism is not simply people rejecting spirituality for materialism. For many people, consumerism is a type of spirituality, even if they do not recognize it as such. It is a way of pursuing meaning and identity, a way of connecting with other people. Many others, finding themselves in relentless pursuit of the requisite material things of the American dream, sense that something is awry. They read reports of Thai women being worked to death making the plastic toys and gadgets that litter our lives, and they recoil. The problem is not people deliberately choosing their own comfort over the lives of others because of their skewed values. The problem is a much larger one: changes in the economy and society in general have detached us from material production, producers, and even the products we buy. I will take each of these in turn.

Production

Take a look around your home or room at the things you and your family own. How many of these items did you make? If you are a typical Westerner, the answer is "very few." Even meals are often prepackaged affairs to be microwaved and consumed. We take this situation for granted; almost all the things we have, we have bought. In most homes in most cultures for most of human history, however, the situation was radically different. Before the advent of industrialization, the typical home was a site of production, not merely consumption. Most people lived on farms, and they made the majority of the goods they used. People had less, and life was often hard. There is no need to romanticize preindustrial society. But the difference in our attitudes toward material things can hardly be overemphasized. We used to make things; now we buy them.

The Industrial Revolution depended on people moving from subsistence farming and handcrafts to factory labor. This was accomplished in several ways. The forced enclosure of common lands in England and the Continent often made subsistence farming untenable. The enclosure movement privatized common lands, dividing them up among landowners, usually to the advantage of large landholders and the detriment of subsistence farmers.[3] Cottage industries were wiped out by the flood of cheap manufactured goods from the new factories, often forcing people

3. For a detailed account of this process in England, see J. L. Hammond and Barbara Hammond, *The Village Labourer 1760-1832: A Study in the Government of England before the Reform Bill* (New York: Harper & Row, 1970).

to seek work in the same factories that put them out of business.[4] The movement from handcrafts to factory work was significant. Today, however, we are even further removed from the production of goods. Fewer and fewer Americans or Europeans have any idea what factory work is like, since the process of globalization has sent many manufacturing jobs overseas, with more such transfers coming every day. Not only do we not make the things we use; more and more, we don't make any things at all.

Why should we care? Perhaps because it has something to do with widespread negative attitudes toward work in our society. "Thank God it's Friday" is a common sentiment, and not only among blue-collar workers. The cartoon *Dilbert* expresses a deep discontent among white-collar cubicle-dwellers as well. Many people do not see their work as meaningful, only a means to a paycheck. One's labor itself has become a commodity, a thing to be sold to the employer in exchange for the money needed to buy things. For many people, work has become deadening to the spirit.

Though negative attitudes toward work are common, it was not meant to be so. Our work was meant to be an outlet for creativity, a vocation to make our impress on the material world. Work is the way we put our very selves into the world of material objects. As Pope John Paul II has said, "Work is a good thing for man — a good thing for his humanity — because through work man not only transforms nature, adapting it to his own needs, but he also achieves fulfillment as a human being and indeed, in a sense, becomes 'more a human being.'"[5] According to John Paul II, work is

4. Rodney Clapp, "Why the Devil Takes Visa: A Christian Response to the Triumph of Consumerism," *Christianity Today* 40, no. 11 (Oct. 7, 1996): 18.
5. Pope John Paul II, *On Human Work* [*Laborem Exercens*] (Boston: St. Paul Editions, 1981), §9. I would have preferred inclusive language, but I have quoted this passage as it appears.

the key to the whole social question, because the question facing society is how to make life "more human."[6] Being more human means, at the same time, participating in the creative activity of God. "The word of God's revelation is profoundly marked by the fundamental truth that man, created in the image of God, shares by his work in the activity of the Creator."[7] This is the true meaning of the call in Genesis to "fill" and "subdue" the earth, and to have "dominion" over it (Gen. 1:28).[8] This spiritual view of work has an evocative appeal to many people who feel alienated from their work and detached from creative engagement with the material world. But this spiritual view of work has not waned simply because people have bad attitudes and negative values; rather, it is because our whole system of production has changed. The system has shown a tremendous capacity to increase the volume and variety of goods produced, while it also detaches us from the creation of things.

Producers

If labor has become a commodity to be sold, it is also a commodity to be bought. The people who make our things are less often ourselves or our neighbors, people with names and faces and aspirations to self-realization, and more often an impersonal "work force." In a reversal of Genesis, "man is treated as an instrument of production, whereas he . . . ought to be treated as the effective subject of work and its true maker and creator."[9] The people who make our things are referred to as "labor costs," which naturally need to be "minimized." And one of the key ways to reduce labor

6. Pope John Paul II, *On Human Work*, §3.
7. Pope John Paul II, *On Human Work*, §25.
8. Pope John Paul II, *On Human Work*, §4.
9. Pope John Paul II, *On Human Work*, §7.

costs is to move production overseas, where wages are much lower and protections for workers are much more lax.

Hip-hop star P. Diddy launched his Sean John line of designer clothing with the slogan "It's not just a label, it's a lifestyle." Of the forty dollars or more that consumers in the United States pay for a Sean John shirt, the women who actually make the shirts, from start to finish, get fifteen cents. Lydda González is a young Honduran woman who worked at Southeast Textiles, a factory in Honduras sewing clothes for Sean John, Old Navy, Polo Sport, and other popular brands. The factory is located in Honduras's San Miguel Free Trade Zone, a compound surrounded by tall metal fences and armed guards. Lydda began working in a bakery at age eleven, and then went to work at Southeast Textiles at seventeen, hoping to pull her family out of poverty. This is what she found instead: miserable wages, twelve-hour shifts six days a week, and mandatory unpaid overtime. She was subjected to random searches, sexual harassment, and compulsory pregnancy tests. Her supervisor was abusive, the air in the factory was filled with textile particles, and the drinking water was tainted with raw sewage. When Lydda and fourteen co-workers got together to demand better working conditions, they were all fired and their names put on a blacklist to be shared with other factory owners. She has been subjected to death threats for speaking out.[10]

Many transnational companies are now pulling out of Central America, but not because of concern for the Lydda Gonzálezes of Honduras. The companies are moving to Asia because they can cut their labor costs in half: instead of the 65 cents an hour Lydda

10. Sarah Stillman, "Made by Us: Young Women, Sweatshops, and the Ethics of Globalization," the 2005 Elie Wiesel Prize in Ethics, at: http://www.eliewieselfoundation.org/EthicsPrize/WinnersEssays/2005/Sarah_Stillman.pdf.

received, they can get away with paying 33 cents an hour in factories in China, with some documented cases of wages as low as 12 cents an hour.[11] Workers making Disney children's books at the Nord Race factories in Guangdong Province, for example, must work 13-15 hours a day, seven days a week, and earn only 33 cents per hour in abusive conditions.[12] Such conditions tend to be the norm, not the exception. The Chinese have even coined a word — *guolaosi* — for death from overwork. A *Washington Post* article highlighted the death of Li Chunmei, a nineteen-year-old woman who collapsed and died after working 16-hour shifts for sixty days straight in a toy factory making stuffed animals for children in the "developed" countries.[13]

We shop; they drop. What is the connection? It's often difficult to find out. The young writer Tom Beaudoin tells a story that many middle-class Westerners can appreciate. He had a vague sense that other people were suffering because of the way his things were made, but he was too busy to know what to do about it. One day he took some of his favorite brand-name items from his closet and decided to call the companies directly to ask how they were made. He often found himself on hold fifteen or more times, as he was routed through various managers, public-relations representatives, even mailroom attendants. On the few occasions that he was allowed to talk to someone knowledgeable about production, that manager would refuse to take responsibility for the well-being of workers, since most production workers

11. Philip P. Pan, "Worked Till They Drop: Few Protections for China's New Laborers," *Washington Post,* May 13, 2002, A01.

12. National Labor Committee, "Disney in China," at: http://www.nlcnet.org/news/china/pdfs/Nord_Race.pdf.

13. Pan, "Worked Till They Drop," cited in Vincent J. Miller, *Consuming Religion: Christian Faith and Practice in a Consumer Culture* (New York: Continuum, 2004), 16-17.

were distanced from the branding company by means of "outsourcing" work to independent contractors.[14]

Naomi Klein argues that the goal of a transnational corporation is a kind of transcendence of the material world. Such a corporation

> attempt[s] to free itself from the corporeal world of commodities, manufacturing and products to exist on another plane. Anyone can manufacture a product, they reason. . . . Such menial tasks, therefore, can and should be farmed out to contractors and subcontractors whose only concern is filling the order on time and under budget. . . . Headquarters, meanwhile, is free to focus on the real business at hand — creating a corporate mythology powerful enough to infuse meaning into these raw objects just by signing its name.[15]

According to Klein,

> . . . after establishing the "soul" of their corporations, the superbrand companies have gone on to rid themselves of their cumbersome bodies, and there is nothing that seems more cumbersome, more loathsomely corporeal, than the factories that produce their products.[16]

We are invited to participate in this transcendence of the material world of production and producers. We are invited to buy products that miraculously appear on store shelves without inquir-

14. Tom Beaudoin, *Consuming Faith: Integrating Who We Are with What We Buy* (Lanham, MD: Sheed & Ward, 2003), pp. ix-xiv.

15. Naomi Klein, *No Logo* (New York: Picador, 1999), p. 22 (quoted in Beaudoin, *Consuming Faith*, p. 69).

16. Klein, *No Logo*, p. 196 (quoted in Beaudoin, *Consuming Faith*, p. 69).

ing into their origins. And yet Beaudoin's dilemma haunts us. As I write this, I stop to look at the clothes I am wearing: my shirt was made in Indonesia, my jeans in Mexico, my shoes in China. My undershirt, whose label instructs me to "have a nice day," was made in Haiti, where a nice day for most people is a day when there is enough food to eat. Most of us would never deliberately choose our own material comfort over the life of another person. Most of us do not consciously choose to work others to death for the sake of lower prices on the things we buy. But we participate in such an economy because we are detached from the producers, the people who actually make our things. Not only are the people who make our things often a world away, but we are prevented from learning about where our products come from by a host of roadblocks. And so we inhabit separate worlds, worlds that have entirely different ways of looking at the material world. The "happy meal" toys from McDonald's that we easily discard reveal nothing of the toil of the malnourished young women who make them. We spend the equivalent of two days' wages for such women on a cup of coffee for ourselves — without giving it a second thought. We do so not necessarily because we are greedy and indifferent to the suffering of others, but largely because those others are invisible to us.

Products

On a road that passes close to the house I grew up in, shopping malls have replaced corn. On one particular stretch stands a new McDonald's fast-food joint, built in a retro style to look like the original McDonald's from the 1950s. Next to it stands a restaurant with a medieval English castle theme, built with drawbridges and turrets. On the other side of the castle is a Mexican fast-food joint, with some features that are meant to suggest an eighteenth-century Spanish mission. It shares space with a seafood restaurant, decorated with a scattering of nets and life preservers and piratey paraphernalia. All of this stands in the middle of an Illinois cornfield.

This kind of scene is so common that it hardly even strikes us as odd anymore. Of course, we know it's all fake. But what would "authentic" mean in this context? We take for granted that other times and places — 1950s America, medieval England, colonial Mexico, the high seas — are all available for our consumption. The expansion of the global economy has brought the world to our fingertips. Music, food, products, and ideas from around the globe are commodities for our enjoyment. This applies not just to low-end products such as fast food, but also to high-culture products such as single-malt Scotch whisky and yoga accessories. Globalization has increased our awareness of, and sympathy for, other times and places. At the same time, however, it produces a detachment from all times and places.

What is "authentic" suburban Illinois culture at the beginning of the twenty-first century? It is, I suppose, fragments of traditional rural Midwestern life and urban Chicago themes, mixed with a hodgepodge of other times and other places. We stand back from culture like a shopper in a supermarket and pick and choose our culture from the infinite variety of experiences marketed to us. Because our consumption can take us anywhere, we are nowhere in particular. The stretch of road I have described is the same as other stretches throughout the country and throughout the world. If you were dropped out of the sky and landed on this road, it would take some investigation to figure out if you were near Chicago or Dallas, Montreal or Sydney.

This detachment tends to characterize our attitudes toward the products we buy. Far from obsessively clinging to our stuff, we tend to buy and discard products easily. We don't make them ourselves or have any connections to the people that make them;

increasingly, we have no connection to the people that sell them either, as small local businesses are replaced by gigantic chain retailers. Under these conditions, our connections to products become very tenuous and fleeting as well. The products we buy are mute as to their origins, and the people we buy them from can tell us little. Products say nothing about where they come from and how they are produced, and we scarcely bother to wonder. We simply take for granted that we can buy fresh bananas in Minnesota in the dead of winter. Meat comes not from cows and pigs but from little Styrofoam trays wrapped in clear plastic. We simply dump them in our carts and keep on shopping.

This does not mean that we have become indifferent to the products we buy. On the contrary, as human relationships fall away from the process of buying products, relationships become more direct between ourselves and our things. The relationship of consumption has largely been reduced to the bare encounter at the store (or on the computer screen) between consumer and thing. But marketers know that consumption could never keep pace with production if encounters with products were encounters with inert things. The product must be made to sing and dance and create a new kind of relationship between itself and the consumer. Over the course of the twentieth century, marketing moved from primarily offering information about a product to associating certain feelings with a product. Soft-drink commercials say little about the actual fizzy liquid that you get when you buy a can; rather, they try to associate the product with positive images like swimsuit-clad youths frolicking on a beach. As one marketer says, "Products are made in the factory, but brands are made in the mind."[17] "Branding" — that is, getting people to identify with a particular corporate brand — is about creating re-

---

17. Quoted in Beaudoin, *Consuming Faith*, p. 76.

lationships between people and things. Associating in one's mind with certain brands gives a sense of identity: one identifies one's self with certain images and values that are associated with the brand. Branding offers opportunities to take on a new self, to perform an "extreme makeover" and become a new person. Some people deal with depression by going shopping; it offers the chance to start anew, to bring something new into one's life. At the same time, branding can also provide a sense of community with all the other people who associate with a particular brand.[18]

Why, then, should we speak about detachment from products when much of consumer culture is about creating relationships with products? Because such relationships are not made to last. There would not be a market for all the goods that are produced in an industrialized economy if consumers were content with the things they bought. Consumer desire must be constantly on the move. We must continually desire new things in order for consumption to keep pace with production. The "extreme makeover" is an ongoing process in the search for novelty, for bigger and better, for "new and improved," and for different experiences. The shaving razor with one blade had to be surpassed by the double-bladed razor, which was bested by three blades, then four, and now an absurd five blades on one razor. This is more than just a continuing attempt to make a product better; it is what the General Motors people called "the organized creation of dissatisfaction."[19] How can we be content with a mere two blades when the current standard is five? How can we be content with an iPod that downloads two hundred songs when someone else has one that downloads a thousand? The economy as it is cur-

---

18. Beaudoin, *Consuming Faith*, pp. 53-58.

19. Quoted in Erik Larson, *The Naked Consumer: How Our Private Lives Become Public Commodities* (New York: Henry Holt and Company, 1992), p. 20.

rently structured would grind to a halt if we ever looked at our stuff and simply declared, "It is enough. I am happy with what I have." The truth is, however, that we do not tend to experience dissatisfaction as merely a negative. In consumer culture, dissatisfaction and satisfaction cease to be opposites, for pleasure is not so much in the possession of things as in their pursuit. There is pleasure in the pursuit of novelty, and the pleasure resides not so much in having as in wanting. Once we have obtained an item, it brings desire to a temporary halt, and the item loses some of its appeal. Possession kills desire; familiarity breeds contempt. That is why shopping, not buying itself, is the heart of consumerism. The consumerist spirit is a restless spirit, typified by detachment, because desire must be constantly kept on the move.

II. Moral Formation and the Material World

Consumer culture is one of the most powerful systems of formation in the contemporary world, arguably more powerful than Christianity. While a Christian may spend an hour per week in church, she may spend twenty-five hours per week watching television, to say nothing of the hours spent on the Internet, listening to the radio, shopping, looking at junk mail and other advertisements. Nearly everywhere we lay our eyes — gas-pump handles, T-shirts, public restroom walls, bank receipts, church bulletins, sports uniforms, and so on — we are confronted by advertising.

Such a powerful formative system is not morally neutral: it trains us to see the world in certain ways. As all the great faiths of the world have attested, how we relate to the material world is a spiritual discipline. As one corporate manager frankly put it, "Corporate branding is really about worldwide beliefs management."[20] This does not mean that the moral effects of consumer culture are always negative. The global economy that has arisen with consumer culture has the potential to broaden our horizons and make us more aware of other peoples and other cultures in the world. Nevertheless, we need to be aware of the powerful formative effects of consumer culture, and we need to approach it with eyes wide open. Let's look at two ways that consumerism constitutes a spiritual discipline, and then at some Christian responses.

Transcendence

Consumerism has certain affinities with the great faith traditions of the world because, as we have seen, it trains us to transcend the material world. Not only do we seek to leave behind the bodily labor that goes into making things. Consumerism represents a constant dissatisfaction with particular material things themselves, a restlessness that constantly seeks to move beyond what is at hand. Although the consumer spirit delights in material things and sees them as good, the thing itself is never enough. Things and brands must be invested with mythologies, with spiritual aspirations; things come to represent freedom, status, and love. Above all, they represent the aspiration to escape time and death by constantly seeking renewal in created things. Each new movement of desire promises the opportunity to start over.

The Christian tradition also recognizes the goodness of material things — and the necessity of transcending them. The basic Christian attitude toward material goods is established already in the opening chapters of Genesis: because all things are created by God, they are good. "God saw that it was good" is a phrase re-

---

20. Quoted in Beaudoin, *Consuming Faith*, p. 44.

peated over and over (Gen. 1:4, 1:10, 1:12, 1:18, 1:21, 1:25, 1:31) in the creation account. But precisely because all things are created by God, created things are not ultimate. Created things, though good, are never ends in themselves; rather, they point outside themselves toward their Creator. As St. Augustine says, all created things contain within themselves traces of the Creator. Precisely because of this, they are not ends but means toward the enjoyment of God. According to Augustine, created things are to be *used,* but only God is to be *enjoyed.*[21]

So the restlessness and dissatisfaction of consumerism are already found in a different form in Christianity. As creatures in time, according to Augustine, we are passionate, desiring creatures, and this is good. The constant renewal of desire is what gets us out of bed in the morning. We desire because we are alive. Created things, however, though essentially good, always fail fully to satisfy because they are not ultimate. They are time-bound, not infinite. Created things fall apart, and we lose interest in them over time. They die. *We* die. Only God is eternal. Only God stops the decay of time. In the words of Augustine's famous prayer to open the *Confessions,* "You have made us for yourself, and our heart is restless until it rests in you."[22] The restlessness of consumerism causes us constantly to seek new material objects. For Augustine, on the other hand, the solution to our dissatisfaction is not the continuous search for new things but a turn toward the only One who can truly satisfy our desires. This does not require the rejection of all earthly things, but an ability to see that all things point to God. People and things are united in one great web of being, flowing from and returning to their Creator. The

21. St. Augustine, *City of God,* trans. Henry Bettenson (Harmondsworth, UK: Penguin Books, 1972), p. 604 [XV.7].

22. St. Augustine, *Confessions,* trans. Henry Chadwick (Oxford: Oxford University Press, 1991), p. 3 [I.1] .

Christian view elevates the dignity of things by seeing them as participating in the being of God; but that view simultaneously causes us to look through and beyond things to their Creator.

Community

Consumerism is a spiritual discipline that, like other spiritual practices, lends itself to a certain practice of community. In identifying with the images and values associated with certain brands, we also identify ourselves with all the other people who make such an identification. Consumerism also allows us to identify with other places and other cultures through our purchases. White kids in Illinois can listen to reggae music and feel themselves in solidarity with the struggles of poor blacks in Jamaica. As Vincent Miller points out, however, such types of "virtual" community tend to reduce community to disembodied acts of consumption.[23] Miller cites the example of Moby's album *Play*, which sold ten million copies in 1999. On that album Moby combines samples of African-American spirituals, gospel, and blues with techno-beat dance music. The song "Natural Blues" begins with a sampling from a 1959 recording of Vera Hall singing "Oh, Lordy, trouble so hard." The sample is chopped and mixed with dance music, and though such samples allow the listener to enter into imaginative sympathy with the struggles of the African-American community in its long hard history, Moby takes the Hall samples out of context and offers them for listener consumption.

Although Vera Hall and the other artists were not even acknowledged, let alone thanked in Moby's liner notes on the *Play*

---

23. Vincent J. Miller, *Consuming Religion: Christian Faith and Practice in a Consumer Culture* (New York: Continuum, 2004), pp. 73-77.

album, *every* song on that album was eventually licensed for use in a commercial — for such companies as Calvin Klein and American Express. Concrete suffering is abstracted from its context and offered as a commodity. No matter how much the listener feels in solidarity with others, *virtual* solidarity offers no concrete results. As Miller notes, "This abstraction impedes the translation of ethical concerns into action, reducing ethics to sentiment. The virtual becomes a substitute for concrete political solidarity, or to put it another way, a fundamentally different act — consumption — is substituted for political action."[24]

In the Christian tradition, by contrast, one's attitude toward material goods is closely tied to an imperative of concrete solidarity with others. When the rich young man approaches Jesus and asks what he must do to attain eternal life, Jesus says to him, "Go, sell your possessions, and give the money to the poor, and you will have treasure in heaven; then come, follow me" (Matt. 19:21). For Jesus, detachment from material goods went hand in hand with attachment to Jesus himself — "follow me" — and to his community of followers. St. Antony of Egypt (251-356) took Jesus' command quite literally. Upon hearing this passage from Matthew's Gospel read in church when he was eighteen, he gave away most of his possessions, sold the rest, and gave the money to the poor. He went off to follow Jesus without the distractions of material possessions, eventually gathering a community of monks around him.[25] St. Clement of Alexandria (150-215) did not interpret Matthew 19 to mean that Christians need to renounce all material possessions, only the ones that are injurious to the soul.[26] Never-

24. Miller, *Consuming Religion*, p. 76.

25. St. Athanasius, *The Life of Antony*, trans. Robert C. Gregg (New York: Paulist Press, 1980), pp. 30-32.

26. St. Clement of Alexandria, "Who is the Rich Man that Shall Be Saved?" §1, 15, at http://www.earlychristianwritings.com/text/clement-richman.html.

theless, Clement also encouraged an attitude of detachment from material things that accompanied a concrete attachment to God and to other people. Clement treated material possessions instrumentally, that is, as a means to be used toward other ends, namely the service of God and others.[27] Things are to be used "more for the sake of the brethren"[28] than for oneself, he said, for "the nature of wealth is to be subservient, not to rule."[29]

St. Thomas Aquinas (1225-1274) derives this attitude of detachment from material things from the fact that God is the proper "owner" of all things. This is a common Old Testament theme: "The world and all that is in it belong to the LORD" (Ps. 24:1).[30] According to Aquinas, humans have dominion over material things only "as regards their use."[31] In other words, this is God's world, and we are just using it for the time being. Any dominion we have over creation is given to human beings in common by God. It follows that, with regard to the power to "procure and dispense" property, an individual has the right to possess property. However, with regard to its use, a person "ought to possess external things, not as his own, but as common, so that, to wit, he is ready to communicate them to others in their need."[32] We may possess property, but use it only for the common good, especially for the sake of the neediest among us.

In the Christian tradition, detachment from material goods means using them as a means to a greater end, and the greater end is greater attachment to God and to our fellow human beings. In

27. Clement of Alexandria, "Who is the Rich Man?" §14.
28. Clement of Alexandria, "Who is the Rich Man?" §16.
29. Clement of Alexandria, "Who is the Rich Man?" §14.
30. See also, e.g., Exod. 19:5: "'The whole earth is mine,' says the LORD."
31. St. Thomas Aquinas, *Summa Theologiae,* trans. Fathers of the English Dominican Province (Westminster, MD: Christian Classics, 1981), II-II.66.1.
32. Aquinas, *Summa Theologiae,* II-II.66.2.

consumerism, detachment means standing back from all people, times, and places, and appropriating our choices for private use. Consumerism supports an essentially individualistic view of the human person, in which each consumer is a sovereign chooser. In the Christian tradition, the use of material things is meant to be a common use, for the sake of a larger body of people. We do not help each other as individuals but as members of one another. According to Paul's famous image (1 Cor. 12), we are all members of the same body, the body of Christ. There is pluralism in the body: some are eyes, some are hands, some are feet. And yet precisely because of that differentiation, all are needed. No member can say to another, "I have no need of you" (1 Cor. 12:21). Furthermore, Paul says, the members of the body who seem weakest are the most indispensable (12:22-24). The poor and the needy are not just objects for individual charity; rather, they are indispensable because they are part of our very body. "If one member suffers, all suffer together with it; if one member is honored, all rejoice together with it" (12:26). The reason that we do not cling to material things is precisely because of our attachment to others. We must constantly be ready to relinquish our claim to ownership, and to use our goods for the common good of the whole body.

III. Being Consumed

There is no question about whether or not to be a consumer. Everyone must consume to live. The question concerns what kinds of practices of consumption are conducive to an abundant life for all. In the Catholic tradition, the Eucharist is a particularly important locus for the Christian practice of consumption. Let's conclude this chapter by considering this sacramental practice and how it might affect our daily practices of consumption.

In the Eucharist, Jesus offers his body and blood to be consumed. "Jesus said to them, 'I am the bread of life. Whoever comes to me will never be hungry'" (John 6:35). The insatiability of human desire is absorbed by the abundance of God's grace in the consumption of Jesus' body and blood. "Those who eat my flesh and drink my blood have eternal life" (6:54), that is, they are raised above mere temporal pursuit of novelty. "Do not work for the food that perishes, but for the food that endures for eternal life" (6:27).

It would be easy enough to assimilate the consumption of the Eucharist into a consumerist kind of spirituality. The presence of Jesus could become another kind of commodity to be appropriated for the benefit of the individual user. Indeed, much of what passes for Christianity in our culture today is addressed to fulfilling the spiritual needs of individual consumers of religion. Many kinds of religion — or more commonly, "spirituality" — are largely about self-help, using God to cope with the stresses of modern life. The practice of the Eucharist is resistant to such appropriation, however, because the consumer of the Eucharist is taken up into a larger body, the body of Christ. The individual consumer of the Eucharist does not simply take Christ into herself, but is taken up into Christ. Jesus says, "Those who eat my flesh and drink my blood abide in me, and I in them" (6:56). Paul writes to the Corinthians: "The cup of blessing that we bless, is it not a sharing in the blood of Christ? The bread that we break, is it not a sharing in the body of Christ? Because there is one bread, we who are many are one body, for we all partake of the one bread" (1 Cor. 10:16-17).

The act of consumption is thereby turned inside out: instead of simply consuming the body of Christ, we are consumed by it. St. Augustine hears God say, "I am the food of the fully grown; grow and you will feed on me. And you will not change me into you like the food your flesh eats, but you will be changed into me."[33] In the Christian view, we do not simply stand apart, as individuals, from the rest of creation — appropriating, consuming, and discarding. In the Eucharist we are absorbed into a larger body. The small individual self is de-centered and put in the context of a much wider community of participation with others in the divine life. At the same time, we do not lose our identities as unique persons, for as Paul says, each different member of the body is valued and needed for the body to function (1 Cor. 12:12-27).

If we remain satisfied with the unity of our own communities, however, we have not fully grasped the nature of the Eucharist. For becoming the body of Christ also entails that we must become food for others. And this often involves moving beyond our own communities and comfort zones. Jesus teaches this lesson in a dramatic way in his depiction of the Last Judgment in Matthew 25:31-46. When the Son of man comes in glory, he will gather all the nations before him and separate those who will inherit the kingdom from those who will be sent into eternal punishment. To the former group he will say: "Come, you that are blessed by my Father . . . for I was hungry and you gave me food, I was thirsty and you gave me something to drink, I was a stranger and you welcomed me, I was naked and you gave me clothing, I was sick and you took care of me, I was in prison and you visited me" (Matt. 25:34-36). When the blessed cannot remember ever attending to Jesus when he was hungry or thirsty, a stranger or naked, sick or in prison, Jesus tells them that, whenever they did it to the least of his brothers or sisters, they did it to him (25:40). Here "brothers and sisters" does not refer merely to Christians, for the Son of man is judging "all the nations" (25:32).[34] All the downtrodden are Christ's broth-

---

33. Augustine, *Confessions,* p. 124 [VII.16].

34. *The New Jerome Biblical Commentary* notes that the term *adelphos*

ers and sisters. To those who are condemned for not attending to Jesus, he says, "Just as you did not do it to one of the least of these, you did not do it to me" (25:45).

What is truly radical about this passage is not that God rewards those who help the poor; what is truly radical is that Jesus *identifies himself* with the poor. The pain of the hungry person is the pain of Christ, and it is thus also the pain of anyone who is a member of the body of Christ. If we are identified with Christ, who identifies himself with the suffering of all, then what is called for is more than just charity. The very distinction between what is mine and what is yours breaks down in the body of Christ. We are not to consider ourselves as absolute owners of our stuff, who then occasionally graciously bestow charity on the less fortunate. In the body of Christ, your pain is my pain, and my stuff is available to be communicated to you in your need, as Aquinas says. In the consumption of the Eucharist, we cease to be merely "the other" to each other. In the Eucharist, Christ is gift, giver, and recipient; we are simultaneously fed and become food for others.

Our temptation is to spiritualize all this talk of union, to make our connection to the hungry a sentimental act of imaginative sympathy. We could then imagine that we are already in communion with those who lack food, whether or not we actually meet their physical needs. We might even wish to tell ourselves that our purchases of consumer goods do in fact feed others — by creating jobs. But we have no way of knowing if such jobs create dignity or merely take advantage of others' desperation unless we

---

(brother) in Matthew sometimes refers to a member of the Christian community and sometimes to "any human being as the object of ethical duty." The commentator concludes that Matt. 25:40 should be taken in the latter sense, noting that the word is dropped in Matt. 25:45. See Raymond E. Brown, Joseph A. Fitzmyer, and Roland E. Murphy, eds., *The New Jerome Biblical Commentary* (Englewood Cliffs, NJ: Prentice Hall, 1990), p. 669.

find concrete ways to overcome our detachment from production, producers, and products.

The first step toward overcoming our detachment is to turn our homes into sites of production, not just consumption. Few of us have the means to make most of what we consume, but simple acts such as making our own bread or our own music can become significant ways to reshape the way we approach the material world. Making things gives the maker an appreciation for the labor involved in producing what he consumes. It also increases our sense that we are not merely spectators of life — for example, hours spent passively watching and listening to entertainment that others make — but active and creative participants in the material world. We can appreciate, as Pope John Paul II said, our true vocation as sharers in the creative activity of God.

Overcoming our detachment from producers is a daunting task when so much of what we need to know is hidden from our view. Nevertheless, there are ways to foster life-giving connections with the resources available to us. One way to do so is to donate time and money to those in need. Another way is to try to ensure that our choices with money contribute to a sustainable life for others. Depositing money in smaller banks that specialize in community development is a simple way to put money to the service of those ignored by most corporate banks.[35] Buying things that are locally produced, and at stores that are locally owned, generally increases the chances of relationship and accountability. There is also a growing Fair Trade movement that ensures fair wages and equitable treatment to producers around the world. The U.S. Catholic bishops, through Catholic Relief Services

35. The Self-Help Credit Union in Durham, North Carolina, is one successful model of small-business and home loans to lower income and minority people (see www.self-help.org).

(CRS), sponsor a program of Fair Trade in coffee, chocolate, and many other handmade items. The goal of the program, according to CRS, is "a new model of international trade built on right relationships between us and the people overseas who create the items we consume — relationships that respect human dignity, promote economic justice, and cultivate global solidarity."[36] Rather than leaving coffee growers to the mercy of "market forces," to middlemen who try to pay them as little as possible, Fair Trade organizations such as CRS ensure a sustainable wage for growers. They also educate American consumers, putting names and faces on those who produce what they consume.[37]

Finally, overcoming detachment from the products we buy is not a matter of developing a fierce attachment to material things. Things are not ends in themselves; they are means to greater attachment to others. We are not to cling to our things, but to use them for the sake of the common good. But to have a good relationship with others, it is necessary to have a proper relationship with things. We must understand where our things come from and how our things are produced. Things do not have personalities and lives of their own, but they are embedded in relationships of production and distribution that bring us into contact, for better or for worse, with other people's lives. A sacramental view of the world sees all things as part of God's good creation, potential signs of the glory of God; things become less disposable, more filled with meaning. At the same time, a sacramental view sees things only as signs whose meaning is only completely fulfilled if they promote the good of communion with God and with other people.

36. CRS Fair Trade at: http://www.crsfairtrade.org/index_flash.cfm.
37. One can take a virtual tour of coffee production in Matagalpa, Nicaragua, at: http://www.crsfairtrade.org/coffee_project/index.htm.

chapter 3

THE GLOBAL AND THE LOCAL

In this chapter, I treat the problem of globalization as a version of the ancient philosophical conundrum of the one and the many. How should the global and the local, the universal and the particular, the one and the many, be related? Along the way I will argue that the process of globalization is not, as the word implies, merely a process of universalization, the dominance of the one over the many, but that it is a peculiar proliferation of the many who are still ultimately absorbed into the one. I will then turn to the great twentieth-century Catholic theologian Hans Urs von Balthasar to argue that only Christ adequately solves the problem of the one and the many. Christ is the key, therefore, to the sustenance of a sane culture in a globalizing world.

I will treat globalization as, in part, an economic and political phenomenon; but, more importantly, I will present globalization as a way of seeing, an aesthetic, that configures space and human subjects in peculiar ways. Implicit in my argument is the conviction that culture and economics are not autonomous spheres with no mutual effect. Economic relationships do not operate on value-neutral laws, but are rather carriers of specific convictions about the nature of the human person — the person's origins and destiny. There is an implicit anthropology and an implicit theology in every economics.

It is possible, for example, to see in globalization a kind of secularized catholicity, a longing for worldwide communion that may have its origins in the Christian desire to bring the Good News to the whole world and unite all human beings as one. There is much in this fragmentary longing that a Christian could recognize as the clandestine work of the Holy Spirit. My purpose in this chapter, however, is to argue that globalization is a way of configuring space that fails to produce a true catholicity, for it abstracts human relations — economic and otherwise — from their concrete embodiment in the local and the particular. The particular is rendered disposable, and the globalizing subject becomes detached from relationships that can render subjectivity possible. Globalization sees the world through homogenizing eyes in a way that ultimately dissolves all differences into the same; this aesthetic is powerful but not unavoidable. I will show how Balthasar presents an alternative aesthetic in the form of Jesus Christ, an aesthetic that constructs human subjects and communities in a different way.

I. The Triumph of the Universal

The term "globalization" is sometimes used as a rough synonym of "whatever is happening in the world these days." I will use it in a somewhat more refined sense to speak of the process of worldwide economic, political, and cultural integration that has taken on accelerated force in the last few decades. Even given this broad definition, however, there is no full consensus on what globalization means or even if it really exists. A group of skeptics believe that globalization is a myth: they begin with a thoroughly economic understanding of globalization as an integrated world market, then argue that there was, in fact, more integration in the nineteenth century under the gold standard. Today, they argue, we have more intervention into the market by nation-states and increasing fragmentation into regional, ethnic, religious, and national blocs.[1]

I will argue that there is truth in the positions of both the globalization affirmers and the globalization deniers, precisely because universalization and fragmentation are two sides of the same coin. I begin with universalization. There is no question that significant shifts have occurred in the movement from a "Fordist" to a "post-Fordist" model of production. In the former model, as championed by Henry Ford, the wheels of production were greased by regarding one's employees as one's consumers. The factory town was an educative enterprise in civic consumption: the concentration and discipline of labor in the assembly line was accompanied by the cooperation of management, union, and family in the production of consumers who were able and willing to buy the products they produced. The demise of Fordism began in the 1970s via the accelerated internationalization of the labor market and the consequent separation of production from consumption. Under pressure from rising oil prices and general overproduction, First-World corporations began moving their operations en masse to countries where cheap labor could be found. The well-documented exploitation of cheap labor in the Two-Thirds World (as I discussed in the first two chapters of this book) is not exactly new under the sun, but the rate at which nationally based corporations became transnational has undergone a tremendous increase in the past thirty years.

1. For a summary of this viewpoint, see David Held, Anthony McGrew, David Goldblatt, and Jonathan Perraton, *Global Transformations: Politics, Economics, and Culture* (Stanford, CA: Stanford University Press, 1999), pp. 5-7.

As a result, the local and the particular have been increasingly integrated into the global market. Locations have become formally interchangeable and measurable according to quantifiable considerations of labor price, availability of raw materials, and laxity of environmental oversight. As the *New York Times* declares, "The new order eschews loyalty to workers, products, corporate structures, businesses, factories, communities, even the nation." The chair of Gulf & Western observes: "All such allegiances are viewed as expendable under the new rules. You cannot be emotionally bound to any particular asset."[2]

The discipline of labor through assembly line and factory town has thus been changed, but labor is not consequently more free. The discipline of labor now depends less on the surveillance of a particular location, and more on the sheer ability to flee. For example, to meet a recent holiday demand for toys in the United States, the Kader corporation was forcing its young female workers in China to work fourteen hours a day, seven days a week. Chinese government officials objected, but as Andy Lee, an executive for Kader, told a *Business Week* reporter, "We told them, this is the toy biz. If you don't allow us to do things our way, we'll close down our Chinese factories and move to Thailand." The Chinese officials backed down.[3] The willingness and ability of capital to abandon any particular location at any time has played a crucial role in subduing wages worldwide and in sapping the ability of unions to gain leverage in negotiations with corporations. Hence unions have begun attempts to go global and organize across national boundaries — without much success.

This detachment from the local and the particular has been fa-

2. Jerry Mander and Edward Goldsmith, eds., *The Case Against the Global Economy* (San Francisco: Sierra Club Books, 1996), p. 221.
3. Robert A. Senser, "Dragon in the Toy Factory: Workers' Rights in Asian Plants," *Commonweal* CXX, no. 17 (Oct. 8, 1993): 12.

cilitated by a series of international agreements that relativize the sovereignty and oversight of national and local governments. NAFTA and the Uruguay Round of the GATT agreements were approved as the elimination of barriers to "free trade." What that means in reality is that the decisions of more local forms of government on environmental protections and health and safety regulations can be overridden without their consent. The GATT created the World Trade Organization (WTO), centered in Geneva, which has the power to declare a local law a barrier to free trade. Any country that does not conform is subject to trade sanctions. One of the first acts of the WTO in the United States, for example, was to target a law passed by the Massachusetts state legislature barring the state government from purchasing products from Myanmar (formerly Burma), home of one of the world's most oppressive military regimes. While the WTO strictly polices local legislation meant to protect workers, local habitats, and so forth, it has increased the protection of corporate property rights.[4] One result has been an increase in the centralization of corporate power, as well as a tendency to concentrate corporate power across geographical frontiers through mergers and acquisitions.

What is meant by "free trade," therefore, is a detachment from the local and a commitment to the hypermobility of capital. This can be seen clearly in the evolution of the financial system. "Banking," says the *Financial Times,* "is rapidly becoming indifferent to the constraints of time, place, and currency."[5] The deregulation of financial activity by the Western nation-states in

4. Nader and Wallach, "GATT, NAFTA, and the Subversion of the Democratic Process," in Mander and Goldsmith, *Case Against the Global Economy,* pp. 92-96.

5. Quoted in David Harvey, *The Condition of Postmodernism* (Oxford: Blackwell Publishers, 1990), p. 161.

the 1970s and 1980s has resulted in the formation of a global stock market, a global commodity and debt futures market, and currency and interest rate swaps. As a result, there has been an acceleration of what is called "paper entrepreneurialism," the making of profits by ways other than the production of actual goods and services. Techniques vary from takeovers and raids of rival corporations (or even unrelated companies) to creative accounting techniques whereby multinational corporations can make profits from small relative shifts in currency values and interest rates across geographic boundaries. The instability of the current financial system is attributable to the way that capital flows are directed and redirected without restraint of time or space.[6] The most valuable asset is information, specifically the kind that allows for a universalizing gaze that maps the whole of the globe as so many interchangeable localities.

The mobility and universalization of transnational corporations has had a profound effect on culture. This effect is obvious to anyone who has had the eerie experience of traveling hundreds, even thousands, of miles without a change of scenery. It is possible to drive from one coast of the United States to the other and eat the same food, stay at the same motel, shop at the same mall, hear the same music on the radio (the same music you were hearing on the radio twenty-five years ago — "classic rock"), hear the news delivered in the same accent, see the same cars, see the same clothes, and hear the same narrow range of political opinions all the way from Florida to Oregon, from California to Maine. Of course, this phenomenon does not just apply to the United States. I have heard "Disco Duck" in Yugoslavia and (to my everlasting shame) eaten at a Pizza Hut in Chile. We are rapidly approaching a utopia, which, says the president of Nabisco, will be "one world

6. Harvey, *The Condition of Postmodernism*, pp. 160-64.

of homogeneous consumption. . . . [I am] looking forward to the day when Arabs and Americans, Latins and Scandinavians will be munching Ritz crackers as enthusiastically as they already drink Coke or brush their teeth with Colgate."[7] Sumner Redstone, owner of Viacom and the purveyor of *MTV* and *Ren and Stimpy* to a waiting world, declares: "Just as teenagers are the same all over the world, children are the same all over the world."[8] Seeing them that way makes them increasingly so.

II. The Particularization of the Universal

The dominant universalization that I have been discussing, however, is not the whole picture, for globalization has also produced a certain proliferation of the particular, which has taken different forms. One form is a kind of opposite reaction to globalization that seeks a retreat and retrenchment in particular identities. Thus the title of Benjamin Barber's book *Jihad vs. McWorld*.[9] It is no secret that the globalization of capitalism and Western culture has spawned a host of what are termed "fundamentalisms" that are sworn to mortal combat against what they usually see as the Americanization of the world.

A second form of particularization is the move toward multi-culturalism, the celebration of diversity we hear so much about at our universities and schools. Here the explicit attempt is not to replace the hegemony of Western culture in a given location with

7. Quoted in Jerry Mander, "The Rules of Corporate Behavior," in Mander and Goldsmith, *Case Against the Global Economy*, p. 321.

8. Quoted in Richard Barnet and John Cavanagh, "Homogenization of Global Culture," in Mander and Goldsmith, *Case Against the Global Economy*, p. 73.

9. Benjamin R. Barber, *Jihad vs. McWorld* (New York: Times Books, 1995).

another hegemony, say Islam, but to affirm the juxtaposition of as many different cultures and faiths as possible within a given space. That is, the idea is not to replace the one with another one, but to replace the one with the many. Where particularities have faded, it is necessary to recover or invent them, which is reflected in the title of the Hobsbawm and Ranger book *The Invention of Tradition*.[10] The contributors to this anthology show how, at the end of the nineteenth century and beginning of the twentieth century, national symbols, monuments, and histories — for example, state Shinto in Japan — were invented as a way of creating a link to the past in an increasingly deracinated world. The invention of tradition is thus an explicitly modern form of anti-modernism. The process continues today in phenomena as diverse as Wicca, Kwanzaa, and Montenegran nationalism.

A third form of the resurgence of the particular is found in the bewildering variety of products and services offered to the consumer, at least in affluent societies. What sociologist George Ritzer has called the "McDonaldization of Society" is not a one-sided process of ever-narrowing choices.[11] McDonald's itself is engaged in a never-ending process of trying to produce novelty, to reconfigure the sizes and sauces of its products to give at least the appearance of something new to attract the consumer. The post-Fordist economy depends on increasingly high rates of turnover, planned obsolescence, and the creation of new desires to stimulate consumption and stave off the specter of overproduction. The Fordist tendency toward vertical integration is replaced by subcontracting, outsourcing, and "just-in-time" delivery that maximize flexibility. Computer technologies permit small-batch

10. Eric Hobsbawm and Terence Ranger, eds., *The Invention of Tradition* (Cambridge: Cambridge University Press, 1983).

11. George Ritzer, *The McDonaldization of Society* (Thousand Oaks, CA: Pine Forge Press, 1993).

production and rapid retooling and reskilling for a constantly changing array of products. Rapid change in production has been matched by rapid change in consumption. Internet shopping has made an entire world of products and services available. Technology and mass saturation marketing have produced an acceleration of changes in fashion and trends. Goods are more disposable than ever. At the same time, there has been a shift toward consumption of services over and above consumption of goods; services are more ephemeral and have a shorter "lifetime."[12] In short, the new economy has made a greater variety of goods and services available than ever before.

Are we left to conclude, therefore, that globalization is the realization of both greater universality and greater particularity? In a sense, this is an accurate way of expressing it. Roland Robertson has coined the term "glocalization" to illustrate how the process simultaneously produces greater sameness and greater difference.[13] However, I think that, if we examine it more closely, such an apparently happy synthesis of the universal and the particular is misleading. There is no question that the new economy has produced an abundance of goods for those who can afford to purchase them. But difference in globalization is largely a surface difference. The sheer abundance of difference, the very variety and speed with which differences are produced, mandates that no difference be sufficiently different to constitute a true departure from the same. Any difference is on the surface and is ultimately dispensable. This applies not only to products but to traditions, cultures, religions, and self-identities of all kinds.

If we examine multiculturalism, for example, it becomes ap-

---

12. Harvey, *The Condition of Postmodernism*, pp. 284-86.

13. Roland Robertson, *Globalization: Social Theory and Global Culture* (London: Sage, 1992), pp. 173-74.

parent that the true battle lines in this culture war are not the diversity of global cultures versus the sameness and hegemony of Western civilization. Both sides are wrong. Multiculturalism is more accurately described as a rival unity, a rival hegemony. Beyond simple and laudable attempts to include those who are different in our institutions, multiculturalism as an ideology is in fact postcultural or anticultural: it subjects every culture to the withering hegemony of cultural relativism and individual choice. As Christopher Clausen observes, "Twentieth-century America is a graveyard of cultures."[14] The melting pot is where cultures come to die, where bagpipes and haggis are traded for Britney Spears and Big Macs, unless one chooses consciously to retain elements of the past. To make a tradition the subject of choice, however, is to kill it as a tradition. Any claim a particular cultural or religious tradition might make on the individual is threatened by the overriding imperative of choice. The result is what Clausen appropriately labels "mass individualism": the more we celebrate our differences for their own sake, the more similar we become.

This same dynamic is observable in the production and consumption of goods. Awash in the bewildering variety of the supermarket — the twenty-four different kinds of orange juice, some with pulp, some without, some with pulp and calcium added, some "homestyle," and so on — it is easy to forget that all that variety tends to fade into the one overriding imperative to consume. The economy, we are told, is driven by demand and not by any substantive *telos* of human good. When we are in a recession, we are told to consume — it doesn't matter what — because buying pushpins or pornography will grease the wheels of pro-

14. Christopher Clausen, *Faded Mosaic: The Emergence of Post-Cultural America* (Chicago: Ivan R. Dee, 2000), p. 7.

duction in equal measure. To stimulate demand and desire, we are presented with ever-differing products — from "clear deodorant" to "dry beer" — that exhibit ever more ephemeral differences. Everything is available, but nothing matters. It is not difficult to feel, as Bruce Springsteen sings, that there are "57 Channels and Nothin' On."

It thus becomes increasingly necessary to convince us that the products we buy are really, as Dodge's one-word slogan has it, "different." Plank Road Brewing Company responds to the large national beer brands with an advertising campaign featuring a couple of down-home folks sitting around the company's garage-sized warehouse. Leinenkugel commercials feature the brewmaster, Jacob Leinenkugel, whose family has been brewing in Chippewa Falls, Wisconsin, for generations. The giant brewer Miller responds with an ad touting the virtues of good old macrobrew: "It's time to drink beer made in vats the size of Rhode Island." What we don't see is that Plank Road and Leinenkugel are both owned by Miller, which in turn is owned by a South African conglomerate. So much for diversity. The surface appearance of diversity in fact masks a stifling homogeneity.

This homogeneity is not just a matter of corporate culture but culture in general. Globalization is an aesthetic, a way of seeing the world, of reading its images and signs. Fredric Jameson is right, I think, to call postmodernism the "cultural logic of late capitalism," because in both it is the surface image that counts. In globalized capitalism, exchange value has overcome use value, and what is desired is desire itself. Postmodernism also trumpets the vacuity of signs, such that the signifier refers only to other signifiers, not to the signified. According to Jameson, postmodernism is a leap in what Walter Benjamin called the "aestheticization" of reality, the cutting loose of representations from what they represent. "Postmodernism is the consumption of sheer commodification as a process."[15] Andy Warhol captured this depthlessness of signs in his Campbell soup-can art. As Jameson observes, Warhol's art should be a powerful political critique of commodity fetishism. The fact that it is *not* makes it postmodern. Even the critique of commodities has itself become a commodity.[16]

III. The Theological Significance of Globalization

The emptying of the particular for the universal is not merely accidentally related to theology, because the reconciliation of the many with the one is perhaps the quintessential religious question. In Christianity the theme of catholicity captures the aspiration of a divided humanity to be united as a whole. Indeed, the Greek words *(kath' holou)* from which the English word "catholic" is derived indicate a universal reach, a taking in of reality "according *(kata)* to the whole," or "on the whole." We speak of someone with "catholic" tastes as someone who ranges broadly, who takes in a little of this and a little of that. In Roman Catholic circles, representatives of universities like to proclaim that their institutions are "catholic with a small *c* " to dispel the fear of crabbed dogmatism. "Catholic" is treated as an antonym of "particular," with the result that "Roman Catholic" appears to be oxymoron.

In the Catholic tradition, however, there is a much more subtle interplay between the particular and the universal in the concept of catholicity. As Henri de Lubac pointed out, there is a sense in which, for the church fathers, catholicity meant a gathering together rather than a spreading out, a cohesion around a cen-

15. Fredric Jameson, *Postmodernism, or, the Cultural Logic of Late Capitalism* (Durham, NC: Duke University Press, 1991), p. x.

16. Jameson, *Postmodernism*, p. 9.

ter that unites the disparate elements in their very diversity.[17] That center is the Eucharist, in which the universal Christ is mediated in particular form. Each eucharistic community is not merely a part of a whole, as if Christ could be divided into parts, but a microcosm, a mini-cosmos in which the cosmic Christ is wholly present. The closer one is attached to the particular community gathered around one particular altar, the more united one becomes to the universal. For this reason Paul can refer to the local assembly in Rome as *hole he ekklesia,* the whole church (Rom. 16:23). "Roman Catholic" turns out not to be an oxymoron after all.

Globalization as I have been describing it often takes the form of a parody of true catholicity. The cosmopolitan gaze ranges broadly, and it sees the attachment to the particular as being in fundamental tension with universality. The particular is thus drained of its eternal significance. This vacuity of the particular image shows up in acute form in the attempts to construct a global theology and thus to deal with the embarrassing particularity of Jesus. The so-called pluralists, such as John Hick, see globalization as an opportunity to shed the oppressive exclusivity of Christian belief in Jesus Christ as the unique mediator of salvation. As the pluralists tell the story, globalization has awakened Christians to the reality that they share the planet with a majority of people who are not Christian and who do not share their beliefs. Arrogant claims by colonists to the superiority of the Christian way have caused bloodshed and misery for the non-Western world. If we are to coexist with others on a shrinking planet, we must learn to appreciate the otherness of the other and the legitimacy of other ways of salvation.

17. Henri de Lubac, *The Motherhood of the Church,* trans. Sr. Sergia Englund (San Francisco: Ignatius Press, 1982), p. 174.

The pluralists' appreciation for the particular is based on an a priori assumption that Lessing was right: there is an ugly and uncrossable ditch between the absolute, on the one hand, and the relativities of history, on the other. Stanley Samartha, a contributor to the Hick and Knitter anthology *The Myth of Christian Uniqueness*, puts it this way: "Through the incarnation in Jesus Christ, God has relativized God's self in history. Christian theologians should therefore ask themselves whether they are justified in absolutizing in doctrine him whom God has relativized in history."[18] The solution to the problem of many religions is to relativize them all in the face of the absolute. Pluralism appeals to the utter mystery and ineffability of God, though even "God," according to Hick, is just a particular Christian name for the "ultimate Reality" to which all religions point. Therefore, Christ, just like the Buddha, is a sign of something else, a pointer to the absolute Reality that lurks mysteriously beyond all signs. As Samartha says, the pluralists thus adopt the solution of the Vedas to the problem of the one and the many: truth *(Sat)* is One, but has many names.[19]

The pluralists claim to have found a way to celebrate the uniqueness of each particular religion without trying to assert the superiority of one over another. As Hick and Knitter say, Christianity "is unique in the precise and literal sense in which every religious tradition is unique — namely that there is only one of it and there is therefore nothing else exactly like it."[20] If the crite-

18. Stanley J. Samartha, "The Cross and the Rainbow: Christ in a Multireligious Culture," in John Hick and Paul F. Knitter, eds., *The Myth of Christian Uniqueness: Toward a Pluralistic Theology of Religions* (Maryknoll, NY: Orbis Books, 1987), p. 69.

19. Samartha, "The Cross and the Rainbow," p. 73.

20. From the preface of Hick and Knitter, *Myth of Christian Uniqueness*, p. vii.

rion of uniqueness is that there is only one of it, however, being precise would mean rephrasing that sentence thus: "Christianity is unique in the sense in which not only every religious tradition is unique, but every individual thing is unique: my right shoe, that chair, this piece of lint, that box of cereal, that can of Diet Pepsi. . . ." In this merely *quantitative* concept of uniqueness, particularities are recognized, but immediately relativized and trivialized by the dominance of the One. Because any path to the One suffices, particularities are interchangeable. Difference is not celebrated but radically effaced. The different religions are just so many different ways of experiencing exactly the same thing, the ultimate Reality that swallows all difference whole.[21]

In an article subtitled "Religious Pluralism in the Age of the McDonald's Hamburger," Kenneth Surin shows how this kind of pluralism is linked to the rise of economic and cultural globalization. Far from ending the period of colonization, globalization furthers the expansion of the cosmopolitan gaze over the face of the globe. Although the Malaysian villager finds it impossible to imagine that she and the wealthy landowner from the same village occupy the same space, the pluralist indulges in the fiction of a "global village" in which all people share a common space and a common experience. The pluralist is above and detached from all particular traditions, and is able to situate them all next to each other and compare them. Hick writes of what happens "when one stands back from one's own tradition to attempt a philosophical interpretation of the fact of religious plurality."[22] As Surin

---

21. On a recent bleary-eyed Saturday morning, the public television show I was watching with my three-year-old son treated us to children singing a peppy song that went: "We're all different but we're all the same." Another song proclaimed, "Everybody's special." It made me nostalgic for watching Wile E. Coyote get an anvil dropped on his head.

22. Hick and Knitter, *Myth of Christian Uniqueness,* p. 34.

puts it, the "Hicks of this world are seemingly a new kind of subject, one that is 'universal' or 'global' in the way that the McDonald's hamburger has become the 'universal' or 'global' food."[23]

The triumph of the universal and the interchangeability of signs in globalization then produce a peculiar kind of subject. In *After Virtue,* Alasdair MacIntyre writes of certain "characters" or social roles that provide a particular culture with its moral definitions: the manager, the therapist, and the bureaucrat figure prominently in MacIntyre's account.[24] For our purposes, we might add the consumer and the tourist as especially evocative of the subject under globalization. The tourist stands detached from all particular times and places and surveys them all from above, as it were. The tourist craves what is different and authentic, but when particular locations make themselves available to the tourist, authenticity and difference are lost. Particularities, especially from the past, are invented for the tourist, but the tourist cannot participate in them. The tourist can go anywhere, but is always nowhere.

The tourist is a type of consumer, a consumer of places. Consumerism is marked by desire with no *telos* other than consumption itself. Particularities are interchangeable. Above all, the consumer consumes; rather than being drawn ecstatically into a larger drama, the consumer empties things into the self. Both the tourist and the consumer try to transcend their own limits and particularity by adopting a universal stance detached from and consuming particularities. But when they do so, the self becomes a kind of empty shell, itself dependent on the constant novelty of the particular for its being, yet itself simultaneously

23. Kenneth Surin, "A Certain 'Politics of Speech': 'Religious Pluralism' in the Age of the McDonald's Hamburger," *Modern Theology* 7, no. 1 (Oct. 1990): 72.

24. Alasdair MacIntyre, *After Virtue,* 2nd ed. (Notre Dame, IN: University of Notre Dame Press, 1981), pp. 27-32.

destroying the particularity of the many, and thus negating its own being.

IV. The Concrete Universal

Resolving this problem of the particular and the universal is a major preoccupation for Balthasar, who proclaims it *the* fundamental philosophical problem and a fundamental experience of all human being. The nonbiblical person experiences his or her self as limited and nonabsolute, not-one. At the same time, that realization engenders a longing to transcend this limitedness and be joined to what is One and absolute. The person thus simultaneously experiences herself as part of a larger whole, yet realizes that she is other than this whole. The primary way of overcoming this problem is to see the particular, the many, as mere appearance, as ultimately unreal and passing away into the One.[25]

In philosophy the problem of the One and the many has come down to a struggle between rationalism and empiricism. Empiricism is seen as a necessary corrective to the devaluation of the particular and the concrete, but rationalism, as Balthasar says, has always been looked on as the higher form of philosophy, because it attempts to overcome the mere brute facticity of the particular by locating the deeper explanation of things in the realm of essence. Thus we get Hegel's grand subsuming of all historical fact under universal reason. In one sense this can be read as the highest form of tribute to the particular, in that Hegel sees every individual fact as a meaningful presentation of reason itself. In another sense, however, Hegel is the ultimate devaluation

---

25. Hans Urs von Balthasar, *The von Balthasar Reader,* ed. Medard Kehl, S.J., and Werner Loser, S.J. (New York: Crossroad, 1982), pp. 97-99.

of the particular, leaving no room for the genuinely creative and singular.[26]

Religious solutions to this problem are equally unsatisfactory, according to Balthasar. They either absorb the One into the many, as in polytheism and pantheism, or, more commonly, they absorb the many into the One, as in Vedic and Sufi mysticism.[27] Any single person who would bring redemption to the estrangement of the many must be some one individual who cannot redeem history as a whole. At best the person could only be a religious founder who points to a universal way of salvation that all may tread. "Any such 'way' could be historical only in an external sense: if it is really to have validity for all, to be a universal and valid way, its basis will have to be in essentiality."[28] Once again, the universal trumps the particular.

Only Christianity satisfactorily solves the problem of the One and the many, because Christ is the "concrete universal." Only in the Incarnation can an individual be universal and the universal be individual. "Christ is neither one individual among others, since he is God and so not susceptible of comparison, nor is he the norm in the sense of a universal, since he is this individual."[29] However, though Christ is not just one individual among others, Balthasar makes clear that he is also not the mere removal of an individual from the sphere of his fellow individuals. Christ is a human being; to raise him above human beings is to make Arius's mistake and thus to eliminate the possibility of our participation

---

26. Hans Urs von Balthasar, *A Theology of History* (New York: Sheed & Ward, 1963), pp. 5-7.

27. Hans Urs von Balthasar, *The Glory of the Lord,* vol. I, trans. Erasmo Leiva-Merikakis (San Francisco: Ignatius Press, 1982), p. 506.

28. Balthasar, *A Theology of History,* 10.

29. Hans Urs von Balthasar, "Characteristics of Christianity," in *Explorations in Theology,* vol. I (San Francisco: Ignatius Press, 1989), p. 170.

in Christ. Christ remains immersed in history; yet, because he is God, all historical norms are subordinated to Christ. Christ cannot be interpreted in terms of the universal norms of history, since he is unique, so there is no place for abstracting from particular cases or inessential accidents. There are no accidents in God, so Christianity can only display the normative content of history manifest in the irreducible particular fact of Jesus Christ. Christ is the concrete norm for all abstract norms. The norm for history comes not from above it, from the absolute laws of universal reason, but from within it.[30] Christ thus bridges Lessing's ditch between the absolute and the particularities of history.

Because Christ is immersed in history and does not merely hover above it, there are some analogies between Christ and some other relatively unique events. A great work of art, for example, is simultaneously universal in its appeal and in its connection to the whole history of art before it, and yet unique and inexplicable in terms of that history and of the influences that preceded it. In love, something of the universal shines forth in one particular individual. Finally, in death one becomes conscious of one's uniqueness and loneliness, despite the solidarity of the human race and the social nature of salvation. All these relative singularities, however, fail to escape the dialectical relationship with the universal. Only Christ is *absolutely* unique: Christ embraces the course of all history in an ultimate way.[31]

The arrogant claim of the Incarnation is thus much more radical than the claim that the one God becomes transparent at particular times and places. The doctrine of the Incarnation, as Balthasar says, is the claim that the "all" has become identical with a tiny "someone." This runs directly counter to the broaden-

---

30. Balthasar *A Theology of History*, pp. 14-21.
31. *The von Balthasar Reader*, pp. 115-20.

ing and universal impulse of other religions, and it casts Christianity in the role of a particularity that "demonically questions the unification of the world."[32] We have here the apparent antithesis of the process of globalization. Balthasar admits that "the future belongs to the 'religious man' who will 'tolerate' the different outward forms religion may take,"[33] while Christianity becomes more solitary. In a passage that strikingly parallels my analysis of the homogeneity of globalization, Balthasar says:

> For faith, all human religions and philosophical systems seem to approach one another ever more closely on one side, and Christianity seems to become more and more isolated on the other. No matter how variegated the market display of human world views may be, seen from a bit of distance its stalls and attractions soon come to take on a common air, all equally of human provenance and human proportions.[34]

But Christ, of course, is not isolated, not merely a unique "freak of nature," because Christ is, precisely *as* unique, the fulfillment of all partial truths contained in the religious myths of the world.[35] As the *absolutely* unique, Christ is the center to which all the relative uniqueness of all the other forms and images of the world are related.[36] Christ is the infinitely integrating one who makes room in himself for everything truly human. Other forms are not simply false and thus excluded; their fragmentary truth is illuminated by the comprehensive truth of

32. *The von Balthasar Reader*, p. 195.
33. Balthasar, "The Word and History," in *Explorations in Theology*, vol. I, p. 38.
34. *The von Balthasar Reader*, p. 114.
35. Balthasar, *The Glory of the Lord*, vol. I, pp. 496-97.
36. Balthasar, *The Glory of the Lord*, vol. I, p. 507.

Christ, and in Christ they are brought fully to themselves. Their differences are not simply obliterated; in them the whole Christ is revealed.

This integration is very different from the way that globalization makes every particular form dispensable, an empty stand-in for a universal desire. What makes the form of Christ attractive is the perfect harmony between finite form and infinite fullness, the particular and the universal. Christ is the unique hypostatic union between archetype and image. Christ does not point beyond himself to something else, something more universal, but he is the fullness of God. For this very reason, Christians reject the Platonist idea that the world of matter is a concealment of the spiritual. To the Platonist concept, according to Balthasar, the sacraments and the church itself are mere material crutches for the materially minded. On the other hand, because of the Incarnation, Christians see the universal revealed in even the lowest of the material. The cross remains revelation — not a mere pointer to something else.[37]

Nevertheless, the appearance of the One in the many is not the limitation of the One. God remains wholly other, and God transcends the many. Even in the natural world, the very existence of what is not one both reveals and conceals the One; on the one hand, the limitedness of what is not one points beyond itself to the possibility of unity. Yet there is no way simply to deduce the One from the many, because, as Balthasar says, we can never understand how a monad would need to go out of itself into a dyad in order to preserve its unity: "In other words, by its very being creation shows that it is not necessary."[38] Therefore, in natural theology the contingency of the many both reveals and conceals

37. Balthasar, *The Glory of the Lord,* vol. I, pp. 432-40.
38. Balthasar, *The Glory of the Lord,* vol. I, p. 448.

God. Only in Christ is the many revealed as "justified" by the very plurality that exists within the triune God himself.[39] God is revealed as *not* a monad. Because the Trinitarian God is both one and not-one, in Christ the One and the many, God and the world, are revealed as not-other *(non-aliud)* to each other. But God is, of course, both not-other and yet remains wholly other.[40] The Incarnation does not resolve, but it brings to perfection, the most complete revelation of God within the most extreme concealment. God is shown immediately in the form of the God-man, and yet he is made manifest in the "hopelessly relativized reality of one individual man in the crowd,"[41] and one who dies an ignominious death besides.

In the pluralist concept of God, it is a one-sided emphasis on God's utter transcendence, his concealment from the many, that licenses the proliferation of particular religious forms, all of which are interchangeable and none of which really reveal the universal. God's hiddenness reveals only the emptiness of signs. In Balthasar's much more complex account, it is precisely God's hiddenness that *reveals* God. This is especially apparent in the cross, which for Balthasar is the *concretissimum*. Nothing could conceal the God of the universe more completely than a half-naked man being tortured to death. And yet the Christian claim is that it is precisely here, in this self-emptying, that the very fullness of God's inner life is revealed, for the Father is only the Father in his complete self-giving to the Son, which is returned by the Son as the Gift, which is the Holy Spirit. Therefore, the ugliness of the cross itself paradoxically *is* pure glory.[42] The particularity of the cross does not limit God, but opens up

39. Balthasar, *The Glory of the Lord,* vol. I, p. 506.
40. Balthasar, *The Glory of the Lord,* vol. I, p. 459.
41. Balthasar, *The Glory of the Lord,* vol. I, p. 457.
42. Balthasar, *The Glory of the Lord,* vol. I, p. 460.

the world to participate in the drama enacted on the stage of the Trinity itself.[43]

The *kenosis* of God creates the possibility of a human subject very different from the consumer self. The absolute uniqueness of Christ cannot be subsumed under any more general categories of being. If God is God, then God must be always beyond our comprehension: *si comprehendis non est Deus*. We are, nevertheless, invited to participate in the Trinitarian life through Christ and the work of the Spirit. But in order to do so, we cannot grasp, we can only submit. We cannot stand back from the world and survey it; we must simply take our role in the drama that God is staging and give ourselves to it.[44]

The aesthetic that accompanies the Christ-form thus produces a particular kind of subject. The aesthetic of *Herrlichkeit* moves necessarily into the dramatics of *Theo-Drama*. Once the person sees the form of Christ, he or she is moved to follow. Unlike the consumer self who consumes, the true self is taken outside itself, enraptured, swept away by the form that is anything but indifferent. Indeed, to speak of a unique human self at all, one must begin outside the self. In living beings, says Balthasar, the problem of the one and the many appears in that every individual member of a species shares in a nature that is identical in every individual, but yet each one possesses it in a unique way. As a spiritual being, however, the human person is not content with this merely *quantitative* distinction of one individual from another. One's uniqueness is encountered in being addressed by an other who finds one indispensable. But this other cannot be merely another human being, for then the recognition could always be withdrawn.

43. Hans Urs von Balthasar, *Theo-Drama*, vol. III, trans. Graham Harrison (San Francisco: Ignatius Press, 1992), pp. 46-47.

44. Balthasar, *The Glory of the Lord*, vol. I, p. 450; see also "Characteristics of Christianity," pp. 172-73.

Without God, there is nothing really unique; the temptation will always be to absorb the individual into the universal, the person into an all-encompassing nature.[45]

What constitutes the human person for Balthasar is not merely being recognized as a self by God, but also being sent out of one's self by God. One's very identity is discovered in one's mission.

> Outside Christ's acting area, no one can identify himself, nor can he be conclusively and validly identified by anyone else. . . . Who knows if he really is a particular, unique individual, or not just anybody, someone who just happens to have individual features: *"Mann ist Mann"*? *En Christoi,* in the acting area Christ opens up as the fruit of his Resurrection, each individual is given a personal commission; he is entrusted both with something unique to do and with the freedom to do it. Bound up with this commission is his own, inalienable, personal name; here — and only here — role and person coincide.[46]

He adds that this personal commission is "actually constitutive of the person as such."[47]

This analysis of the human person is dependent on the analysis in *Theo-Drama* on the person of Christ, who reveals humanity to itself. As God's exhaustive self-communication, Christ's mission is identical with his person. Balthasar's exegesis of New Testament texts, especially from John, shows how Jesus' knowledge of himself coincides with his knowledge of being sent. And this

---

45. *The von Balthasar Reader,* pp. 90-92.
46. Balthasar, *Theo-Drama,* vol. III, p. 51.
47. Balthasar, *Theo-Drama,* vol. III, p. 51.

analysis of God's economy in Jesus of Nazareth flows from Balthasar's analysis of the immanent Trinity. Existence as receptivity to being sent out receives its form from the procession of the Son from the Father, and the openness of the Son to being sent in time to the world by the will of the Father.[48] What's more, the mission of Christ is also the very form of self-emptying, in which he who is in the form of God is abandoned to the cross. God thus makes room within himself for human freedom, susceptibility to temptation, and even death, thus making it possible for human beings to participate in the drama of Christ. "Thus, in the very discipleship in which the Christian 'loses his soul', he can attain his true identity."[49]

The true identity of each unique human person is thus founded on the overcoming of an illusory self-sufficiency through the overcoming of the opposition between the One and the many, God and creatures.

Just as the divine Persons do not confront one another as autonomous beings but, in God's one concrete nature, are forever one divine Being, so too, in Christ, the covenant between God and creature as a covenant of free partners is forever surpassed and indissolubly established, in anticipation, upon the hypostatic union. . . . This becomes most striking for us in the Eucharist: in it the whole substantial Christ offers himself to the world as the gift of the Father, and he establishes the Christian's total life of faith upon the physico-sacramental "eating and drinking" of his Flesh and Blood.[50]

---

48. Balthasar, *Theo-Drama*, vol. III, pp. 149-57; see also *A Theology of History*, p. 25.

49. Balthasar, *Theo-Drama*, vol. III, p. 162.

50. Balthasar, *The Glory of the Lord*, vol. I, p. 480.

The form of this eating and drinking is established not by human beings but by Christ: in its entirety the event and person of Christ is eucharistic, given and poured out to be consumed by others. If in consuming the Eucharist we become the body of Christ, then we are called, in turn, to offer ourselves to be consumed by the world. The Eucharist is wholly *kenotic* in its form.[51] To consume the Eucharist is an act of anticonsumption, for here to consume is to be consumed, to be taken up into participation in something larger than the self, yet in a way in which the identity of the self is paradoxically secured.

Thus Balthasar says that self-giving in the Eucharist participates in the very life of the Trinity. The "flowing" of Christ into the Eucharist is "the glowing core about which . . . the cosmos crystallizes, or better, from which it radiates."[52] Nevertheless, this center is a decentered center, for the Eucharist "enables him to give himself away so prodigally that, by the power of the Holy Spirit, he is 'liquified' and rendered accessible to all times and places, without forfeiting his uniqueness."[53] This universalization of the body of Christ, however, is never detached from the local and the particular, for the eucharistic community is essentially local, gathered around the altar in a particular time and place. Furthermore, the particular is of supreme importance because the Eucharist is not a mere sign that points to Christ; this particular piece of bread *is* the body of Christ.

> The eucharist is the marvelous means of freeing Christ's historical humanity from the confines of space and time, of multiplying mysteriously its presence without forfeiting its

51. *The von Balthasar Reader,* pp. 282-84; *The Glory of the Lord,* vol. I, pp. 573-74.

52. *The von Balthasar Reader,* p. 284.

53. Balthasar, *Theo-Drama,* vol. III, pp. 38-39.

unity and, since it is given to each Christian as his indispensable nourishment (John 6:53-58), of incorporating all into the body of Christ, making them in Christ one body through which courses the divine life. Through the eucharist the Church comes into being as the body of Christ; and while the one flesh of the Lord is multiplied, mankind divided is unified in it.[54]

The catholicity of the church is not sustained by a cosmopolitan detachment from the particular, the (lowercase) "catholic taste" of the globalized subject. "Catholic" means a gathering rather than a spreading out, a unification of the many through attachment to the local eucharistic community. One becomes more catholic, more universal, the more one is tied to a particular community of Christians gathered around the altar. As Balthasar says,

> The *Catholica* is in fact a region whose middle point is everywhere (where the Eucharist is celebrated); and (structurally) she can theoretically be everywhere: geographically, her periphery extends to "the very ends of the earth" (Rev. 1:8), a periphery that in any case can never be far from the midpoint.[55]

V. Conclusion

I have argued here that globalization is an aesthetic and a practice that fails to solve satisfactorily the problem of the one and the many. As a result, a consumer subject and a homogenizing culture

54. Balthasar, "The Word, Scripture and Tradition," in *Explorations in Theology*, vol. I, pp. 15-16.
55. Balthasar, *Explorations in Theology*, vol. IV, trans. Edward Oakes (San Francisco: Ignatius Press, 1995), pp. 65-66.

become increasingly common features of our world. I have suggested that Balthasar's analysis of Christian aesthetics and dramatics can provide a way of overcoming the dualism of universal and particular without collapsing the latter into the former. If Christ is the concrete universal, then it suggests an aesthetic in which the particular is given its particularity precisely by incorporation into the universal. The subject becomes a subject by being sent out of the self. The form of human life is then not consumption but *kenosis*. However, this *kenosis* is not mere altruistic self-emptying but participation in the infinite fullness of the Trinitarian life. If economic relations are not to be excluded in the drama of divine-human relations, then the form of economic life is the life of the Trinity, which is mutual self-giving and mutual receiving.

Though Balthasar himself never draws out the economic and social implications of this aspect of his work, the implications are profound. If detachment from particular places and communities has contributed to the depersonalization of the global economy, then a proper aesthetic of the particular would place the human person back at the center of economic relations, as Pope John Paul II has repeatedly insisted. An aesthetic and practice of self-giving mutuality would likewise resist the construction of the subject as consumer, which equally depersonalizes the subject by disrupting the divine *eros*, which marks true human flourishing.

All of this can only be instantiated in concrete, local practices. For it is only in the encounter with other persons that Christ is encountered, in the concrete and not the abstract, and only by attachment to — not detachment from — the concrete that the universal Christ is encountered. The call to Christians is not so much either to embrace or try to replace abstractions such as "capitalism" with other abstractions. It is rather to sustain forms of economy, community, and culture that recognize the universality of the individual person.

One example of how Christians are meeting this call is Church Supported Agriculture (CSA), which creates a direct link between family farmers and local congregations. Rather than limit their economic activism to demanding that the state intervene in the market, local churches are creating alternative kinds of economic spaces in which they resist the abstraction of globalization by face-to-face encounters between producers and consumers. In the CSA model, family farmers — most of whom farm organically and practice environmentally sustainable methods — sell their produce directly through local congregations. Parishioners either buy individual products or buy a share of a farmer's produce at the beginning of the season, thus helping share in the risks of farming. The church serves as a drop-off point for produce and a place for farmers and parishioners to meet. In this space they avoid the middleman and they personalize the food. Food no longer comes from some anonymous distant place; rather, it comes from another particular human being, and the consumer enters into a relationship with that producer. In this encounter, the person is seen as another self and another Christ, the universal in the particular. As a result, economic exchanges are not based simply on supply and demand, on what the market will bear. This model sets prices to ensure a sustainable living for farmers, who are otherwise subject to the vagaries of the market.[56]

However, the engagement with the concrete, treating the neighbor as another self, is not restricted to geographic proximity. The Fair Trade movement I discussed in Chapter 2 is an example of how Christians can be global in a way that does not lead to detachment from the local. Fair Trade recognizes that the poor in faraway countries are our neighbors; they, too, are members or

56. For one example of Church Supported Agriculture, see www. wholefarmcoop.com.

87

potential members of the body of Christ. Fair Trade treats the distant neighbor not as "labor costs," reducible to monetary terms, the universal standard of exchange. Fair Trade sees the distant neighbor in all of her or his particular dignity: a person with concrete needs, one whose particular pains and joys are shared by the other members of Christ's body, which is simultaneously global and local.

Jesus Christ's incarnation, death, and resurrection situates the subject in a drama in which the subject is united to particular others in the body of Christ. This body opens up the possibility of forms of exchange that are based neither on self-interest nor self-sacrifice but on seeing the concrete other as not-other, as part of the same body. The Christian is called not to replace one universal system with another, but to attempt to "realize" the universal body of Christ in every particular exchange.

chapter 4

SCARCITY AND ABUNDANCE

There was a woman named Rosalinda with whom I attended Sunday mass when I lived in Santiago, Chile, in the 1980s. Rosalinda lived in a small wooden shanty with her elderly mother. Their income, which sufficed for little more than bread and tea, was derived from the potholders and other items that Rosalinda crocheted and sold at the local market. On one of my first visits to her home, Rosalinda gave me a little crocheted bird that is used for grasping the handles of hot teakettles. When Rosalinda presented it to me as I was leaving her home, my first impulse was to reach into my pocket and give her some money for it. But I sensed that that would have been the wrong thing to do.

The little blue-green bird with a white fringe currently adorns the rice container on my kitchen counter. I live with my wife and kids a world away from Santiago in St. Paul, Minnesota. We live our lives at the intersection of two stories about the world: the Eucharist and the market. Both tell stories of hunger and consumption, of exchanges and gifts; the stories overlap and compete. In this concluding chapter, I will try to tell these two stories briefly, and reflect on what they mean for Rosalinda and the bird.

I. Hunger and the Market

Economics, we are told, is the science that studies the allocation of resources under conditions of scarcity. The very basis of the market, *trade* — giving up something to get something else — *assumes scarcity*. Resources are scarce wherever the desires of all persons for goods or services cannot be met. In other words, hunger is written into the conditions under which economics operates. There is never enough to go around. But it is not simply the hunger of those who lack sufficient food to keep their bodies in good health. Scarcity is the more general hunger of those who want more, without reference to what they already have. Economics will always be the science of scarcity as long as individuals continue to want. And we are told that human desires are endless.

This insight about desire is not new. For St. Augustine, the constant renewing of desire is a condition of being creatures in time. Desire is not simply negative; our desires are what get us out of bed in the morning. We desire because we live. The problem is that our desires continue to light on objects that fail to satisfy, objects on the lower end of the scale of being that, if cut off from the Source of their being, quickly dissolve into nothing.[1] The solution to the restlessness of desire is to cultivate a desire for God, the Eternal, in whom our hearts will find rest.

In a consumer-driven market economy, the restlessness of desire is also recognized. Marketing constantly seeks to meet, create, and stoke new desires, often by highlighting a sense of dissatisfaction with what one presently has and is. In a consumer culture, we recognize the validity of Augustine's insight: particular material things cannot satisfy. Rather than turning away from material

---

1. Augustine, *Confessions,* trans. Henry Chadwick (Oxford: Oxford University Press, 1991), pp. 29-30 [II.10].

things and toward God, in consumer culture we plunge ever more deeply into the world of things. Dissatisfaction and fulfillment cease to be opposites, for pleasure is not in possessing objects but in their pursuit. Possession kills *eros;* familiarity breeds contempt. That's why shopping itself has taken on the honored status of an addiction in Western society. It is not the desire for any one thing in particular, but the pleasure of stoking desire itself, that makes malls into the new cathedrals of Western culture. The dynamic is not an inordinate attachment to material things, but an irony and detachment from all things. At the level of economics, scarcity is treated as a tragic inability to meet the needs of all people, especially those who are daily confronted with death because of hunger and extreme deprivation. At the level of experience, scarcity in consumer culture is associated with the pleasurable sensation of desiring. Scarcity is implied in the daily erotics of desire that keeps the individual in pursuit of novelty.

For a number of reasons, desire in consumer society keeps us distracted from the desires of the truly hungry, those who experience hunger as life-threatening deprivation. It is not simply that the market encourages an erotic attraction toward things, not persons. It is that the market story establishes a fundamentally individualistic view of the human person. The idea of scarcity assumes that the normal condition for the communication of goods is through trade: to get something, one must relinquish something else. The idea of scarcity implies that goods are not held in common, that the consumption of goods is essentially a private experience. This does not mean that charitable giving is forbidden, but it is relegated to the private realm of preference, not justice. One can always send a check to help feed the hungry, but one's charitable preferences will always be in competition with one's own endless desires. The idea of scarcity establishes the view that *no one* has enough. My desires to feed the hungry are always being distracted by the competition between their desires and my own.

Adam Smith thought that this distraction was a result of the fact that every person is "by nature, first and principally recommended to his own care."[2]

> Men, though naturally sympathetic, feel so little for another, with whom they have no particular connexion, in comparison of what they feel for themselves; the misery of one, who is merely their fellow-creature, is of so little importance to them in comparison even of a small conveniency of their own.[3]

In his *Theory of Moral Sentiments,* Smith ponders the question of how disinterested moral judgments could ever trump self-interest. He developed the idea that pain and other sentiments are communicable from one individual to another via the ability of the human person sympathetically to put himself or herself in the position of another. Nevertheless, according to Smith, nature has made our resentment of a lack of justice greater than our resentment of a lack of benevolence, so only the former is subject to punishment: "When a man shuts his breast against compassion, and refuses to relieve the misery of his fellow-creatures, when he can with the greatest ease . . . though everybody blames the conduct, nobody imagines that those who might have reason, perhaps, to expect more kindness, have any right to extort it by force."[4] Society can exist without benevolence, but not without justice.[5] In the absence of explicit violence or theft, the inability of a person to

2. Adam Smith, *The Theory of Moral Sentiments,* ed. A. L. Macfie and D. D. Raphael (Oxford: Oxford University Press, 1976), p. 82 [II.ii.2.1].

3. Smith, *The Theory of Moral Sentiments,* p. 86 [II.ii.3.4].

4. Smith, *The Theory of Moral Sentiments,* p. 81 [II.ii.1.7].

5. Smith, *The Theory of Moral Sentiments,* pp. 85-91 [II.ii.3].

feed herself is not a failure of justice but a call for benevolence, which falls to individuals. The communicability of pain in the body of society is faint. Moral indignation in its strong form is reserved for explicit attacks on the status quo of life and property. Adam Smith does not simply leave the care of the hungry to individual preference, however, for in the larger scheme of *The Wealth of Nations*, the needs of the hungry are addressed by the providential care of the market. According to Smith, the "invisible hand" of the market guides economic activity so that the pursuit of self-interest by uncoordinated individuals miraculously works out to the benefit of all. The great economic machine of society is driven by people's wants. Through the mechanism of demand and supply, the competition of self-interested individuals will result in the production of the goods society wants, at the right prices, with sufficient employment for all at the right wages for the foreseeable future. The result is an eschatology in which abundance for all is just around the corner. In the contemporary consumer-driven economy, consumption is often urged as the solution to the suffering of others. Buy more to get the economy moving, because more consumption means more jobs; via the miracle of the market, my consumption feeds you. One story the market tells, then, is that of scarcity miraculously turned into abundance by consumption itself, a contemporary loaves-and-fishes saga.

In reality, however, consumerism is the death of Christian eschatology. There can be no rupture with the status quo, no inbreaking kingdom of God, but only endless superficial novelty. As Vincent Miller says, "Since desire is sustained by being detached from particular objects, consumer anticipation wishes for everything and hopes for nothing."[6] The witness of the martyrs

---

6. Vincent J. Miller, *Consuming Religion: Christian Faith and Practice in a Consumer Culture* (New York: Continuum Books, 2003), p. 132.

to living the kingdom of God in the present becomes a curiosity: How could someone be so committed to some particular thing as to lose his life for it? We are moved by the suffering of others, but we can hardly imagine a change radical enough to undermine the paradigm of consumption. Even the suffering of others can become a spectacle and a consumable item: tsunamis sell newspapers.[7]

And so we choose to believe that, through the miracle of free competition, our consumption will feed others. But the truth is that self-interested consumption does not bring justice to the hungry. The consumer's pursuit of low, low prices at Wal-Mart means low, low wages for the people in Asia who make the products we buy. Eschatological hope easily fades into resignation to a tragic world of scarcity.

II. Hunger and the Eucharist

The Eucharist tells another story about hunger and consumption. It does not begin with scarcity, but with the one who came that we might have life, and have it abundantly (John 10:10). "Jesus said to them, 'I am the bread of life. Whoever comes to me will never be hungry'" (John 6:35). The insatiability of human desire is absorbed by the abundance of God's grace in the gift of the body and blood of Christ. "Those who eat my flesh and drink my blood have eternal life" (6:54); they are raised above mere temporal longing for novelty. And the body and blood of Christ are not scarce commodities; the host and the cup are multiplied daily at thousands of eucharistic celebrations throughout the world. "Everything that the Father gives me will

7. See Miller, *Consuming Religion*, pp. 133-34.

come to me, and anyone who comes to me I will never drive away" (6:37).

This invitation to come and be filled is assimilable to private spiritualities of self-fulfillment if it is packaged as an "experience" of divine life. But the abundance of the Eucharist is inseparable from the *kenosis,* the self-emptying, of the Cross. The consumer of the body and blood of Christ does not remain detached from what he or she consumes, but becomes part of the body: "Those who eat my flesh and drink my blood abide in me, and I in them" (6:56). The act of consumption of the Eucharist does not entail the appropriation of goods for private use, but rather being assimilated to a public body, the body of Christ. As Augustine reminds us, God is the food that consumes us.[8] The Eucharist effects a radical decentering of the individual by incorporating the person into a larger body. In the process, the act of consumption is turned inside out, so that the consumer is consumed.

When we consume the Eucharist, we become one with others and share their fate. Paul asks the Corinthians, "The bread that we break, is it not a sharing in the body of Christ?" (1 Cor. 10:16). He answers: "Because there is one bread, we who are many are one body, for we all partake of the one bread" (10:17). St. John Chrysostom comments on this passage:

> ... because he said A SHARING IN THE BODY, and that which shares is different from what it shares in, he removed even this small difference. For after he said A SHARING IN THE BODY, he sought again to express it more precisely, and so he added FOR WE, THOUGH MANY, ARE ONE BREAD, ONE BODY. "For why am I speaking of sharing?" he says, "We are that very body." For what is the bread? The

8. Augustine, *Confessions,* p. 124 [VII.16].

body of Christ. And what do they become who partake of it?
The body of Christ; not many bodies, but one body.⁹

The enacting of the body of Christ in the Eucharist has a dramatic effect on the communicability of pain from one person to
another, for individuals are now united in one body, connected
by one nervous system. Not only can the eye not say to the hand
"I have no need of you" (1 Cor. 12:21), but the eye and the hand
suffer or rejoice in the same fate. "If one member suffers, all suffer
together with it; if one member is honored, all rejoice together
with it" (12:26). For this reason, Paul tells the Corinthians that
we should take special care for the weakest members of the body
(12:22-25), presumably because the whole body is only as strong as
its weakest member.

This communicability of pain underlies the obligation of the
followers of Christ toward the hungry. The point of the story of
the final judgment in Matthew 25:31-46 is not simply that an individual performing good deeds — such as feeding the hungry — will
be rewarded with a ticket to the kingdom. The force of the story
lies in the identification of Christ with the hungry: "For *I* was hungry and you gave me food" (25:35). The pain of the hungry person is
the pain of Christ; therefore, it is also the pain of the member of
Christ's body who feeds the hungry person. Unlike in Adam
Smith, there is no priority of justice to charity here, no prior sort-
ing out of who deserves what before benevolence can take place. In
Matthew, as in Paul, the hungry and the benevolent are confused in
Christ, so that distinctions between justice and charity, public and
private, become impediments to seeing reality as God sees it.

9. St. John Chrysostom, *Homily on I Corinthians*, no. 24, in *The Eucharist: Message of the Fathers of the Church*, ed. Daniel J. Sheerin (Wilmington, DE: Michael Glazier, 1986), p. 210.

Adam Smith's economy underwrites a separation between contractual exchanges and gifts. Benevolence is a free suspension of self-interested exchange. As such, benevolence cannot be expected or even encouraged on the public level, because the market functions for the good of all on the basis of self-interested consumption and production. Benevolent giving freely transfers property from one to another; nevertheless, it respects the boundaries between what is mine and what is yours. In the eucharistic economy, by contrast, the gift relativizes the boundaries between what is mine and what is yours by relativizing the boundary between me and you. We are no longer two individuals encountering each other either by way of contract or as active giver and passive recipient. Without losing our identities as unique persons — Paul's analogy of the body extols the diversity of eyes and hands, heads and feet — we cease to be merely "the other" to each other by being incorporated into the body of Christ. In the Eucharist, Christ is gift, giver, and recipient. We are neither merely active nor passive, but we participate in the divine life so that we are fed and simultaneously become food for others.

Our temptation is to spiritualize all this talk of union, to make our connection to the hungry a mystical act of imaginative sympathy. We can thus imagine that we are already in communion with those who lack food, whether or not we meet their needs. Matthew is having none of this: he places the obligation to feed the hungry in the context of eschatological judgment. Paul, too, places neglect of the hungry in the context of judgment. At the eucharistic celebration in Corinth, which included a common meal, those who eat while others go hungry "show contempt for the church of God and humiliate those who have nothing" (1 Cor. 11:22). Those who thus — in an "unworthy manner" — partake of the body and blood of Christ "eat and drink judgment against themselves" (11:27, 29). Those of us who partake in the Eucharist while ignoring the hungry may be eating and drinking our own damnation.

The Eucharist places judgment in the eschatological context of God's in-breaking kingdom. There is no gradual, immanent progress toward abundance that the market, driven by our consumption, is always about to — but never actually does — bring about. The Eucharist announces the coming of the kingdom of God now, already in the present, by the grace of God. Vatican II's *Sacrosanctum Concilium* affirms the eschatological dimension of the Eucharist in these terms: "In the earthly liturgy we take part in a foretaste of that heavenly liturgy which is celebrated in the Holy City of Jerusalem toward which we journey as pilgrims...."[10] In the Eucharist, God breaks in and disrupts the tragic despair of human history with a message of hope and a demand for justice. The hungry cannot wait; the heavenly feast is now. The endless consumption of superficial novelty is broken by the promise of an end, the kingdom toward which history is moving and which is already breaking into history. The kingdom is not driven by our desires, but by God's desire, which we receive as the gift of the Eucharist.

The Economy of Communion Project of the Focolare Movement goes a long way toward making this vision of abundant economic life a reality. Focolare is one of the international ecclesial movements in the Roman Catholic Church, founded by laypeople in Italy amidst the wreckage of World War II. Focolare has recognized that the essence of human life is living in communion. The Economy of Communion grew out of this insight. Beginning in 1991, Focolare began sponsoring ordinary, for-profit

---

10. *Sacrosanctum Concilium* 8, in *Documents of Vatican II*, ed. Austin P. Flannery (Grand Rapids: Eerdmans, 1975), p. 5.

businesses that divide their profits in three equal parts: a third for direct aid to the poor, a third for educational projects that further a culture of communion, and a third for the development of the business. Today more than 700 businesses worldwide follow this model — and thrive.[11]

The Economy of Communion is based on breaking down the divide between people on which economic exchanges are usually based. If we see employees and members of the wider community as members of our own body, then we will make decisions with the well-being and development of those employees, the community, and the environment in mind. The founder of Focolare, Chiara Lubich, has said: "Unlike the consumer economy, based on a culture of having, the economy of communion is the economy of giving."[12] However, the Economy of Communion does not see the poor whom they assist as passive recipients of charity, but as active participants in the process. They contribute their experience of God's love, and most are motivated to share the help they receive with others who are more needy. In turn, recipients become givers, so that the line between recipient and giver is blurred. A Brazilian participant in the Economy of Communion explains:

> It is not merely a question of reaching the right persons and of giving priority to the most urgent needs.... It also involves making sure that the assistance be part of a fraternal rapport that does not tolerate positions of inferiority and superiority

11. Luigino Bruni and Amelia J. Uelmen, "The Economy of Communion Project," *Fordham Journal of Corporate and Financial Law* XI, no. 3 (2006): 645-50. For more information on the Economy of Communion, see www.edc-online.org.

12. Chiara Lubich, quoted at: http://www.edc-online.org/uk/_idea.htm (Nov. 10, 1991).

because it sees the other person as "another me," as a brother, and this is possible due to the fact that we are dealing with persons who know how to share.[13]

If I look at it in that light, I think I can see why it would have been wrong to give Rosalinda money for the bird. It would have annulled the gift and turned it into an exchange. It would have re-established the boundaries between what is hers and what is mine, and therefore reinforced the boundaries between her and me. The Eucharist tells a different story about who we — the hungry and the filled — really are, and where we are going.

13. Margarida Silveira Silva, quoted in Bruni and Uelmen, "Economy of Communism Project," pp. 653-54.

Index

Index

Index